JOHN

G000146969

LEFT TO DIE

GOD'S AMAZING LOVE FOR A REFUGEE WOMAN

but
loved
by
God

malcolm down
PUBLISHING

Contents

Acknowledgements

No book gets completed without the cooperation of many people. This work is no exception. I would therefore like to thank the following:

My thanks go to my wife, Louise, for standing with me in good times and in bad.

Sincere thanks to my publisher, Malcolm Down, for believing in me and in this message – and for making the book a reality at such a crucial time in our history.

To Sarah, for persevering with 'that' front cover

To Ian McCalmont, for proof reading this manuscript in the middle of the night.

To Sheila Jacobs, a fussy but truly brilliant editor, and someone every author wants on their team.

My appreciation also to all the team at Print Planet, Church Road, Holywood, Co. Down. Nothing was a problem – even the lending of a laptop charger on deadline day. (Thanks so much, guys!)

Finally, to all the wonderful people I have met throughout my own journey, including the many who gave me testimonies for this manuscript. God bless you all!

John McCreedy
October 2015

A Brief Outline of the Bible Story of Hagar and Ishmael

As the sun set on Sarai's already beautiful complexion, heads began to turn. Even the king, Pharaoh, was left reeling at the sheer beauty of this stunning Hebrew princess as she, accompanied by her husband, Abram, arrived in Egypt.

Abram and Sarai (their names where later changed to Abraham and Sarah) were viewed as God's 'chosen couple' and their entrance to Egypt certainly didn't go unnoticed. They may not have appeared wearing the normal Egyptian attire; even so, Sarah's exquisiteness could not be concealed.

They'd gone to Egypt following a famine in their own land, and events commenced amidst a background of lies, lust, revenge and a regrettable deception by Abraham which would promptly change the course of all of their lives.

Waiting for them in Pharaoh's palace was another Middle Eastern beauty – Hagar – Egyptian by birth, and a person who would go on to play a pivotal part in the lives of both Abraham and Sarah.

It's assumed Hagar, who was one of the more established and privileged Egyptian slaves in Pharaoh's domain, was instantly given as a gift to Abraham along with sheep and cattle after Pharaoh's roving eye spotted Sarah and he became infatuated with her.

Although advancing in years, Sarah was still stunning to look at and Pharaoh recognised this. So, he began to fantasise about the prospect of having her as his wife, and his officials were promptly sent to take her as the latest addition to the king's collection of spouses.

Abraham, though, had lied to Pharaoh when he and Sarah first showed up in Egypt, telling him Sarah was his sister and not his half-sister and wife, and this is what led to Pharaoh's unrealistic advances towards Sarah in the first place.

It was a lie which produced severe implications.

When God afflicted Pharaoh and his palace with diseases to protect Sarah from Pharaoh, Abraham's dishonesty was finally uncovered. The king quickly put two and two together, realised something was not right and, when he established what had taken place, promptly threw Abraham, Sarah and Hagar out of Egypt.

This upheaval was only the beginning of Hagar's troubles, however. Years later, while in Canaan, Hagar agreed to help both Abraham and the barren Sarah by giving birth to a child, Ishmael, but during her pregnancy Hagar was so badly treated by Sarah she fled into the wilderness.

Two beautiful women battling for the affections of one man is always a recipe for disaster, and this love triangle proved to be no exception.

Following a visitation by God's angel, Hagar obeyed God and returned to give birth to Ishmael, yet she was later heartlessly cast out of the house by Abraham and Sarah and banished to the wilderness of Beersheba along with her now teenage son after the birth of Sarah's son, Isaac.

For the second time in her life, Hagar had clearly lost everything, including the comfort and security of her home. Having experienced the trauma and transition of being uprooted to a culture and religion she didn't understand, when expelled from Egypt by Pharaoh, now she had to adapt to the awful pain of being rejected by Abraham and Sarah from a home both she and Ishmael had become accustomed to.

Naturally, Abraham was troubled at Sarah's request to evict Hagar and Ishmael. Like any good father, he'd prayed for Ishmael and he'd probably grown to love Hagar too! So Sarah's demands meant Abraham faced something of a major dilemma. Ishmael was, after all, Abraham's son... his own flesh and blood... but, in the end, Hagar and Ishmael were banished from the house and made to wander through the unforgiving wilderness of Beersheba.

The name Ishmael was given by God through his angel, and stands as an enduring reminder of God's mercy, because Ishmael means 'God hears'. He will respond in your times of need. Nowhere is this provision more apparent than in the life of Ishmael's mother, Hagar, who not once, but twice, is visited by an angel and rescued at the point of death.

Having been abandoned by Abraham and Sarah, Hagar's world appeared to have imploded – until, miraculously, God stepped in. Equipped with very little food and just a bottle of water, the prospects for this poor Egyptian mother and her son were incredibly bleak until the angel drew near to Hagar and said: 'What aileth thee, Hagar? Fear not; for God hath heard the voice of the lad where he is' (Genesis 21:17).

A well of water was provided and thereafter God helped both Hagar and Ishmael, who settled in the wilderness of Paran where Ishmael became an expert with the bow, the spot where God had provided a well of water for Hagar in her darkest hour.

Just as God had promised, many years before, out of Ishmael, a new nation was born and, against enormous odds, Hagar and her son had survived. The young Egyptian slave girl who ran out of water had eventually found a huge well.

Introduction:
Have You Been Left to Die?

Have you been left to die?

Have you experienced rejection, hurt, betrayal, or exclusion?

Has the colour of your skin, your spiritual upbringing, your marital status or some other issue brought estrangement and disappointment from the place you least expected – your family, friends, and even your spiritual home?

Have you given everything for the cause of an employer, a business venture or a place of worship, only to be cast aside as though you didn't exist?

Instead of finding encouragement, perhaps you've suffered the opposite – a sad sequence of maltreatment and even segregation that has left you feeling totally abandoned.

There are many people like this in the world today. People, who've been subjected to cruel rejection, endured religious discrimination and racial abuse, suffered slavery, faced defining moments and had the awful misfortune of being displaced and separated from their families.

This was the experience of Hagar and her young son, Ishmael. The family members they lived with and served faithfully for many years ultimately betrayed them. In short, they were left to die by a husband and a father (Abraham) and his unsympathetic wife (Sarah).

They were totally forsaken by the only family they possessed. They were rejected and unloved by, of all people, God's people!

Jonathan Swift wrote: 'We have just enough religion to make us hate, but not enough to make us love one another.'[1]

While Hagar has often been overlooked in the book of Genesis in favour of more prominent characters such as Abraham and Sarah, she still gained God's attention in a remarkable way and her story has much to convey to many of the rejected and ill-treated people of the world we currently live in.

Today thousands have been left to die in trucks, on boats and on trains, even on motorways. The global refugee crisis is adequate proof of this – a catastrophe that has seen masses displaced and made homeless throughout the world. The German chancellor, Angela Merkel commented in August 2015 that in the world today we have more refugees than at any time since World War Two.[2]

However, Hagar and her son are testimony that even in the worst of circumstances, God cares about the rejected, the refugee and the homeless person – and God can meet our needs no matter how drastic the situation may appear.

In this account of her life, I do not wish to concentrate on Hagar as a point of theology, but on Hagar the refugee and a person whom God loved exceptionally. I trust this arrangement of events in her life will also present God as He really is – a God of compassion, a God of the impossible and a God of true restoration; not a vengeful, elitist God. Not a God who forces Himself on us, but One who lovingly, gently and subtly finds a way to enter our hearts – regardless of which background we originate from.

I have deliberately chosen the narrative of Hagar and Ishmael because I believe it has an extremely important message to reveal to people in the twenty-first century.

This is a truly magnificent picture of how the love of God can impact all cultures and all religions. It's also a thrilling tale of how the goodness and faithfulness of God can counteract the thoughtlessness of humanity, and appear when we need it most. I have been motivated to write this book through Hagar's brokenness and sorrow, through the rejection she and Ishmael suffered at the hands of chosen representatives of God Himself and, due to the remarkable way God came to their aid when others walked away.

This project didn't solely emerge from study, however, but due to a combination of extremely testing events in my own life, hence I do earnestly pray that the book will prove helpful to others.

Primarily, however, the content challenges people everywhere to embrace ethnic unity from a biblical perspective and reach out to others who are different to themselves. It encourages reconciliation and also seeks to remind people that, no matter which background they belong to, or how they've been disregarded in life, God is for them, God loves them and has a wonderful purpose for their lives.

Notes

1. Jonathan Swift, *Thoughts on Various Subjects*, 1711. (https://ebooks. adelaide.edu.au/s/swift/jonathan/s97th/)

2. See: http://www.telegraph.co.uk/news/worldnews/europe/ serbia/11829354/Angela-Merkel-calls-on-EU-to-help-Western-Balkans-face-migrant-influx.html.

One:
Slavery Then and Now

God Almighty has put before me two Great Objects, the suppression of the Slave trade and the Reformation of Manners. (William Wilberforce)[1]

Having watched the movie *12 Years a Slave* it's impossible not to be extremely moved by the incredible true story of one man's fight for survival and justice. In the pre-Civil War United States, Solomon Northup, a free black man from upstate New York, is abducted in Washington DC in 1841 and sold into slavery. Facing incredible brutality, Solomon struggles not only to survive, but also to retain his self-esteem.

A free African-American man, Northup works as a violinist and resides in Saratoga Springs, New York. Providing he agrees to travel to Washington DC, he is promised a job as a musician, but following his arrival, Northup is drugged and sent to a slave pen along with others who have been deceived and captured in the same way. It's hard to describe the pain he then endures, both from a personal perspective and the inconceivable events he witnesses thereafter. Nevertheless, in the twelfth year of his haunting experience, a fortuitous meeting with a Canadian abolitionist alters his situation and brings to an end his nightmare at the hands of his evil masters. Remarkably Solomon Northup is eventually freed and is emotionally reunited with his wife and children.

The film, which was voted best movie in 2013 and won three academy awards, is an adaptation of the 1853 memoir, *12 Years a Slave*, and illustrates just how horrific human cruelty and slavery can be.

The Russian novelist Fyodor Dostoyevsky stated: 'People speak sometimes about the bestial cruelty of man, but that is terribly unjust and offensive to beasts, no animal could ever be as cruel as a man, so artfully, so artistically cruel.'[2]

Many of the scenes in the movie *12 Years a Slave* bear testimony to the above quote. They are scarcely watchable, such is the meanness displayed by one human being against another; yet the film highlights intensely just why slavery is such a tragic and unacceptable matter. Sadly such violence has even been justified in the name of religion or God, yet God's heart breaks when He witnesses the cruelty of one human being towards another and especially when it is carried out in the name of God.

Blaise Pascal said: 'Men never do evil more completely and cheerfully as when they do it from a religious conviction.'[3]

Much has been written about Hagar in relation to slavery, some of which is supposedly exaggerated, but any point is well made when it highlights injustice and terrible suffering – something Hagar and her son, Ishmael, unquestionably experienced during their own troubled lives. Yet it is helpful to differentiate between slavery in ancient times and the slavery which occurs in our modern era, especially if we are to get an accurate picture of how slavery is impacting our world today.

Back in ancient Middle Eastern culture, for example, slavery was so common that God's laws made provision for its safe and fair practice. It's important to highlight that the term 'slave' had many different meanings during Bible days, and slavery was very different to today.

For example, a slave could be a servant, a bondman or woman – a courtier, who was a humble, willing servant, as Onesimus was to Paul in the New Testament. But the word 'slave' could also mean someone held in bondage, like Joseph in the book of Genesis, sold into slavery by his brothers who hated him. This led to vulnerability when Joseph, who refused the advances of his masters' wife, was accused of rape and was punished by being sent to prison.

In those days a master was not permitted to kill a slave, even if he or she so desired. Instead, they had to think of other ways to dispense with the slave. Slaves were looked after because it made economic sense to keep them alive and functioning, to protect what was usually a significant investment, made with a view to a long-term arrangement.

People often lived at close quarters with their slaves, and saw them as lower status, expendable family members. If debt was the reason for a man becoming a slave, he had a special status, and had to be treated as a hired servant. Every seven years, when the Year of Jubilee came, all such slaves had to be given their freedom. Deuteronomy chapter 15 records: 'If your brother, a Hebrew man or a Hebrew woman, is sold to you, he shall serve you six years, and in the seventh year you shall let him go free from you' (Deuteronomy 15:12, ESV).

Slaves were often foreigners who had been captured in war and bought in an open market or allocated to soldiers of the victorious army. There were also house-born slaves, children born to a woman who was already a slave – her child then automatically belonged to her master. If a slave girl was criminally assaulted, compensation was paid to her owner, not her. A father could sell his daughter as a concubine.

The question is, of course, what would Hagar's slavery have been like in ancient Egypt? She probably would have been comfortable in her abundant Egyptian surroundings, conversant with the Egyptian culture, and familiar with the political and religious system in Egypt, which was totally different to the much more primitive and impoverished lifestyle she would later encounter with Abraham and Sarah.

Of course, slavery of varying degrees has been around for millennia, and throughout the centuries it has existed in virtually every country. The conquered have been made to serve the conqueror, the weak to serve the strong, and the poor to aid the rich. Freedom and prosperity has been the privilege of the few, not the many.

Slavery is an economic fact, not a new phenomenon. Sadly, despite the passing of time it still exists for monetary purposes – and, has become conspicuously more gruesome in our modern world than in Bible days. In the words of the writer Nikki Giovanni: 'There are two people in the world that are not likable: a master and a slave.'[4]

Despite being illegal in every country, slavery somehow still exists, and, significantly, is on the rise again. Yet how does modern slavery differ from historical slavery? Today there are more slaves than ever and very few people are willing to robustly defend slaves any more.

Considerable corruption and crime continues within this

trade. Many even believe government corruption is a leading cause of the persistence of slavery. Slaves are also cheaper than ever and can generate high economic returns. Servitude has always existed where it's been economically beneficial to those in power. Sadly, for these same reasons, slavery continues to occur in the modern world, only this time in a much more sinister way. Why is this important?

In Bible days, slaves were seen as valuable assets and viewed as 'long-term investments', but this is no longer the case.

Many women are forced into the sex trade and made slaves with a view to a high rate of return over a relatively short period of time. Then, often addicted to drugs they have been forced to take, and almost certainly in the country illegally, with no support or proof that they ever existed, a tragic result is more or less assured.

Slavery today differs to Bible days in other ways, too. Whereas a slave was released from a debt after every six years in ancient times, today they are put on 'a long lease' which they cannot bring to an end and so can't leave their employer.

Migrant workers who are smuggled into their new country must pay off their debt – leaving them unable to break free for fear of being deported. Child slavery and marital slavery through forced marriage and buying women for marriage is also vast throughout the world today.

Slavery, therefore, has categorically changed and has become nothing short of brutal bondage which, of course, is why we must question the moral justification for it.

It's why films like *12 Years a Slave* are made, to draw attention to such awful practices. The film may well be tough to watch, but it uncovers a hugely important issue – the unacceptability of slavery.

In the words of Abraham Lincoln: 'If slavery is not wrong, nothing is wrong.'[5]

Significantly the Hebrew name 'Hagar' means 'one who flees' or 'one who seeks refuge'. Hagar and her son, Ishmael, therefore is the story of millions of exploited, trafficked, disabled and rejected people and children throughout the world today. They are fleeing from all kinds of nasty situations and people but, as he did with Hagar, God hears their cries and He feels their pain.

Notably the Bible doesn't disclose if Hagar was born into slavery or if she had been forced into it for the payment of a debt, but it's safe to assume that Hagar's lifestyle while serving under the influence of Pharaoh would have been reasonably secure. Many slaves achieved wealth and high status in Hagar's day. Others were forced to work in less pleasant surroundings. The latter would not have been Hagar's experience at this point in her life. Hagar's freedom, of course, may have been restricted – after all, she was a slave – but she would have been privileged, serving in the splendour of Pharaoh's palace.

Picture Hagar carrying out her duties amidst the opulence of the royal court. She would have mingled daily with other women wearing splendid clothes and intricate jewellery. Like a butler or domestic employee who serves the US President at the White House in America, or the Royal Family at Buckingham Palace in London, she would have valued the lavish surroundings she was labouring in. Due to the nature of her work and location, Hagar would undoubtedly have been entitled to certain privileges and perks and would have moved through eye-catching corridors and witnessed the magnificence of Pharaoh's palace.

In ancient times, a pharaoh's palace included audience

chambers, eating stations, festival halls, extensive gardens and grounds, administrative offices, a library, kitchens and numerous storerooms. The palace ceilings were supported by beautifully carved columns painted to venerate great pharaohs from the past. These were spectacular and outstanding to behold. The interiors were filled with beautiful furniture and pottery. The palace also incorporated quarters for the other members of the royal family. Favoured and esteemed officials, including 'respected slaves', could avail themselves of these facilities frequently.

Exactly how Pharaoh's fortress seemed in Hagar's time is uncertain, but we can assume it would have been impressive in its own right.

By contrast today, many slaves in our so-called 'progressive' modern world exist in appalling conditions, being hugely undervalued as people and personnel.

Several black American feminists have written about Hagar, comparing her story to those of slaves in American history. Wilma Bailey, in an article entitled: 'Hagar: A Model for an Anabaptist Feminist?'[6] refers to her as 'maidservant and slave'. She sees Hagar as a model of 'power, skills, strength and drive. In *Just A Sister Away* and an article, 'A Mistress, A Maid and No Mercy'[7], Renita Weems argues that the relationship between Sarah and Hagar exhibits 'ethnic prejudice exacerbated by economic and social exploitation'.

Are things really any different today?

Millions of people are racially discriminated against and socially exploited by ruthless establishments, and this downward trend appears to be more and more acceptable. The rich are getting richer and the poor are becoming poorer. The current employment market illustrates this all too well. Numerous employers in many countries think nothing of paying young people or foreign nationals well below the minimum wage in a bid to maximise profits. These unscrupulous organisations expect their employees to work an exhausting amount of shifts in unacceptable conditions – conditions they themselves would refuse to toil in. The stresses and strains of having to earn a living in such harsh circumstances, and raise families simultaneously, are naturally considerable. Foreign immigrants are especially vulnerable to this sort of abuse throughout the world, and sadly many of them have succumbed to it due to having no other choice.

Do we spare a thought for the millions of modern-day Hagars who have been forced into such a life, especially single mothers? The odds are stacked against them. They work long hours to survive and then come straight home to deal with the pressing needs of their children. Many of these low-paid workers don't even own their own home, so they find themselves having to relocate their families continually just to secure rented accommodation. They are never sure how long they will have a roof over their heads. This practice is taking place in so-called 'prosperous nations', not just what we tend to view as Third World countries.

Slavery has been defined in the Oxford Dictionary as: 'a person who is excessively dependent upon or controlled by something' or as 'someone who works very hard without proper remuneration or appreciation'.[8] Slavery makes people desperate for freedom. It's not God's intention for men and women to become slaves to sin, slaves to others and especially slaves to political and religious establishments. Satan's house is never a free house. Jesus said: 'if the Son sets you free, you will be free indeed' (John 8:36, NIV 1984).

When God sent his Son, Jesus Christ, it was to liberate all slaves from bondage, both physically and spiritually. Speaking in the book of Luke, Christ Himself proclaimed: 'The Spirit of the Lord is upon me, because he hath anointed me to preach the gospel to the poor; he hath sent me to heal the brokenhearted, to preach deliverance to the captives, and recovering of sight to the blind, to set at liberty them that are bruised' (Luke 4:18).

The great defender of the vulnerable, British politician and philanthropist William Wilberforce, who contributed momentously to the abolishment of the slave trade in Britain during the nineteenth century, said, 'God Almighty has put before me two Great objects, the suppression of the Slave Trade and the Reformation of Manners.'[9]

Even though Wilberforce had written an essay on slavery many years previously, he had to wait until just three days before his death in 1833 to learn that slavery in British colonies would finally be abolished. Almost 200 years later, sadly slavery is well and truly alive! The desire to be free is still tragically the ambition of millions of oppressed, abused and rejected people. Notwithstanding Hagar's story can bring hope and comfort to such people; moreover, her story summons us to believe that all is not lost when God is present.

For further thought, prayer and reflection

- What is the difference between slavery in Bible days and slavery today?
- What would the conditions have been like for Hagar as a slave?
- Are you willing to do anything to help prevent slavery in your area or around the world?
- There are groups to contact such as Antislavery International, founded in 1839, its one of the world's oldest human rights organisations and the only charity in the UK seeking to end all forms of modern slavery. The William Wilberforce Trust provides follow-on support for the women who have been trafficked into sexual exploitation

and are living independently in London. If you currently employ foreign immigrants or young people, are they paid a salary which is acceptable? Do you feel convicted about this? Do you know any foreigners you could employ and help financially?

- If you attend a church are there any people who are being discriminated against which you could help protect and be a blessing to? Why not hold a special prayer time for these individuals and their families inviting them along to see how much you and God cares for them.

- Are you personally a slave to a person, a job, a habit, or a religious establishment or political system?

Notes

1. bbc.co.uk. Last updated 5/7/11.
2. https://www.goodreads.com/author/quotes/3137322.Fyodor_Dostoyevsky
3. Blaise Pascal, Pensées (London: Penguin Classics, 1995).
4. inspirational stories.com.
5. Abraham Lincolnonline.org.
6. The Mennonite Quarterly Review 68 (April 1994), pp. 219–228.
7. Renita J. Weems, *Just a Sister Away* (Philadelphia: Innisfree Press, 1988).
8. oxforddictionaries.com.
9. bbc.co.uk. Last updated 5/7/11.

Two:
Incidents Happen

'Please say you are my sister, that it may be well with me for your
sake, and that I may live because of you.'
(Genesis 12:13, NKJV)

They say accidents happen.

So do incidents.

Prior to the end of an era, and before any major transformation, something has to occur: an incident, a storm, an interruption; a shift of seismic proportions is required in order to propel people to another level and into a path they ought to have found for themselves.

Incidents can and do change our lives. They are no respecter of persons. Whether we like it or not, incidents bring change. If left to ourselves, of course, most of us would willingly stay in the same place forever. No one likes change. It can be a terrible prospect and, more often than not, we require time to adjust to it. People resist change at all costs. Frequently, however, it's not general transformation we resist, but instant adjustment that we fear. We are frightened of what we're unfamiliar with and, let's be honest, change generates a fear of the unknown. Upheaval is always harder to accept when it's unexpected; when you don't see it coming and it catches you off guard.

Has the direction of your life ever been permanently changed due to one single incident? Have you had your world altered beyond recognition, and look back and wonder what on earth happened? We hear about it all the time. A loved one is taken suddenly, a clash on the rugby field leaves a sportsperson paralysed for life; an extramarital affair leaves a spouse devastated and living alone, someone is informed they are losing their job, another is told they have a terminal illness. Events can and do change our lives in both negative – and positive – ways.

Due to a major occurrence in her own life and, because of the actions of someone else (in this case Abraham), overnight Hagar found herself completely uprooted from a culture she was familiar with to a lifestyle she didn't recognise. Change ruthlessly rearranged her existence, but not in the way she'd anticipated. One single incident had callously restructured her daily routine and changed her world forever.

After Pharaoh had discovered Abraham was telling lies when he'd announced Sarah as his sister instead of his half-sister and wife (Genesis 12:11–13), both he and Sarah were immediately deported from Egypt, taking the slave girl Hagar with them.

Countless Bible characters faced similar upheaval and transforming situations which proved to be out of their control. For example, one infamous episode reshaped the world of Joseph in the book of Genesis. After his brothers betrayed him by selling him to the Ishmaelites as a slave, he went from being a happy-go-lucky dreamer in the land of Israel to living in slavery in Egypt, culminating in a long-term prison sentence. Many years later, another more positive episode brought Joseph's release from the very same prison. When the king couldn't find anyone to explain his dreams, Joseph was unexpectedly called out of his cell and, due to his ability to interpret dreams, solved the problem for the king. So grateful was the king that Joseph was immediately appointed Prime Minister and became the saviour of Egypt during a prolonged famine.

A comparable defining moment changed the life of a young man named Mephibosheth in the second book of Samuel. Lame on his feet from infancy, he is located in Lo-debar, a location described in the Bible as a 'place of nothing', when King David sent for him after he discovered that Mephibosheth, the grandson of his former antagonist Saul, was still alive. Having lived in poverty and total obscurity for most of his life, suddenly Mephibosheth was invited to the palace of the king to eat bread and drink wine at the king's table continually. The Bible records: "Then King David sent, and fetched him out of the house of Machir, the son of Ammiel, from Lodebar (2 Samuel 9:5). David then went on to say to Mephibosheth: 'Do not fear, for I will show you kindness for the sake of your father Jonathan, and I will restore to you all the land of Saul your father, and you shall eat at my table always' (2 Samuel 9:7. ESV). One person, one defining moment, one major intervention had irrevocably changed Mephibosheth's surroundings. He never returned to poverty.

The apostle Paul experienced his own life-changing incident on the Damascus Road. The book of Acts says that in his younger days, Saul, as he was called then, was involved in persecuting Jewish followers of Jesus because he believed they were heretics. This persecution actually resulted in the death of many believers. Blinded by a great light, however, Saul was visited by God who transformed him from a persecutor of Christians into one of the greatest Christians who ever lived. Saul was travelling to the city of Damascus when he saw a bright light and heard Jesus' voice saying: 'Saul! Saul! Why do you persecute me?' (Acts 22:7, NIV 1984) He fell to the ground, blinded. Later, after a visit from the Christian disciple Ananias, he recovered his eyesight and began to preach Jesus. Even his name was changed from Saul to Paul as he went from being a follower of Judaism to a principal proclaimer of Christianity.

Sometimes we don't allow for incidents in life or for the Lord to guide our way. The Bible says: 'A man's heart plans his way, But the LORD directs his steps' (Proverbs 16:9, NKJV).

Life-changing incidents are not always welcome and can be very distressing experiences. But they are frequently necessary, not only to move us on from dry and stale places, but to develop within us character – and to get us to where God intended for us to be.

That's not suggesting that God is the author of bad intentions. God is a good God and the author of everything good, but we can always be confident that He brings positive out of the negative incidents which happen in our lives. 'And we know that all things work together for good to those who love God, to those who are the called according to His purpose' (Romans 8:28, NKJV).

Incidents can make or break us. They rock our world, and often when we least expect it. Some incidents are so horrific it can take us years to recover and we often focus on that 'one incident' which came out of nowhere and reshaped our lives.

Open a newspaper or switch on the news and every day we are made aware of incidents which have changed the course of either the life of an individual or a group of people. The rise of fanatical terrorism has left behind some horrendous life-changing consequences for many people today – the 9/11 killings being one of the most graphic illustrations of how sudden events are so often outside of our control. This unimaginable occurrence changed the world forever, especially in relation to security at airports and in major cities. It also changed the world's opinion of Muslims.

For example, due to the horrific nature of this event and, of course, the brutal actions of ISIS terrorists and other radical Muslim groups since, ordinary Muslims are today rejected, feared and disliked by people of other religions. They are often viewed with major suspicion and left to feel like 'outcasts'. They can't hide from this rejection due to their identifiable religious attire. Peaceful Muslims are now known for being persecuted and targeted by their own people. J.K. Rowling was quoted in the Guardian as saying: 'eight times more Muslims are killed by Islamic terrorists than non-Muslims'.[1]

At a time when millions of ordinary Muslims need to be shown love and understanding, instead they are being estranged by people from other faiths due to the dastardly incidents caused by Islamic terrorists.

This rejection is not representative of a just and merciful God, of course, who loves the Muslim just as much as He loves the Christian. Neither is this condemnation of ordinary Muslims fair.

Jesus said: 'Do not judge according to appearance, but judge with righteous judgement' (John 7:24, NKJV). In other words, do not discriminate against a person because of the behaviour of another.

Peaceful Muslims shouldn't be despised because of the actions of Islamic extremists. If you are reading this book as a non-Muslim, can you open your heart to consider the daily prejudice and rejection they may be going through? Due to the immense media scrutiny of Islamic extremists such as ISIS, the stigma and the isolation they feel must be considerable, especially in Western countries.

I know exactly how it feels to be stigmatised because of the actions of terrorists and so do many of my fellow countrymen. Many years ago when the IRA were bombing and killing both Protestants and Catholics in Northern Ireland and blowing up parts of mainland Britain during the period known as the Troubles, lots of Northern Irish people like myself were not well received by some ill-informed individuals on the mainland, people who were clearly unable to distinguish between normal Irish and British citizens living in Northern Ireland, and dedicated terrorists like the IRA. Naturally these people were frightened of being bombed and killed by the terror group, something which is perfectly understandable, but sadly they just heaped everyone into the same basket when it came to Irish people.

I still recall the humiliation we used to suffer arriving at Heathrow Airport in London. I was a British citizen, carrying a British passport, and I had no love for the IRA, or any paramilitary organisation for that matter, having witnessed many of my friends and countrymen killed by such groups; yet, when all of us disembarked from our Belfast plane, we were herded like cattle into a room to be searched and interrogated by British security forces. This was a regular experience in those days for anyone travelling from Belfast to London.

Long before extensive security measures at airports were compulsory following 9/11, lengthy queues were the order of the day as we all waited to clear customs and continue our journey to London or elsewhere. Passengers travelling from other destinations were able to disembark from their flights and continue hassle-free, without any security checks, because they were travelling from another part of the UK or elsewhere.

Those of us travelling from Belfast, however, had to endure the most degrading and lengthy wait to enter the airport arrivals hall. Having completed security, we would then approach what was dubbed the 'walk of shame' – a long narrow corridor where we would frequently experience dirty looks, be called offensive names and made to feel like second-class citizens. I still recall being spat at once by an angry individual who had clearly reached the irrational conclusion that everyone arriving from Belfast must be a terrorist.

Irish people who had lived and worked in England for years and contributed to the economy there complained of being isolated. Of course, this is what happens when people generalise – it becomes easy to judge everyone in the same way. In this case, some allowed their prejudice to obscure their perspective and an entire people-group were rejected because of the actions of a minority.

Isn't this exactly what Muslims are encountering today? And all because of that tragic and inconceivable incident in New York, and the resulting violence from Islamic extremists since in many different countries! Incidents do not only change circumstances, but also our perceptions, and sometimes for the better.

The dreadful image of a three-year-old Syrian boy (Alan Kurdi), discovered dead on a European beach in September 2015, altered many people's perceptions of refugees once and for all. For years displaced people were seen as 'migrants' but not necessarily as refugees. These unfortunate souls were totally unwanted and in recent times disgracefully associated with 'swarms' and 'cockroaches'. Alan Kurdi's picture changed this mindset totally.

Unexpectedly compassion gripped many people in Europe and in the UK – especially in the nation of Germany which led the way in helping almost a million stranded refugees find sanctuary in their country. The powerful picture of the lifeless body of an innocent child on a Turkish beach reverberated across the globe and painted a thousand words. This single predominant incident destroyed, in a moment, centuries of racial prejudice, making it possible for a new compassion and understanding to emerge.

The tragic shooting of people at the Charleston Emanuel African Methodist Episcopal Church in 2015 in the USA is another sad example of just how a single moment can alter the entire course of many people's lives. Dylann Roof, a young white man, walked into a Bible study at an historic black church and was welcomed with open arms as a stranger. Taking advantage of the well-known hospitality of this sanctuary, he mingled with the parishioners, none of whom had any idea that nine of them would be dead within an hour. They lost their devoted pastor who was one of those killed, and many precious members of their church. They entered a Bible study together, but when they came out, they knew things would never be the same again.

In July 2015, in West Sussex, England, a 79-year-old retired lawyer accidently clipped another car in what was described as a very minor traffic accident. As the grandfather attempted to explain what had happened, the driver of the hit car stabbed him multiple times and he died at the scene of the accident. This frenzied attack ended in fatal circumstances for an elderly man, who it was reported hadn't committed any great crime.

In April 2015, many people were going about their business in Nepal assuming things wouldn't change too much when one momentous event shook the entire country. A huge earthquake measuring a magnitude of 7.8 affected apparently over 8 million people – almost a quarter of the entire population of this country. Over 9,000 people were reportedly killed and up to 23,000 injured. None of these individuals, of course, got up on the morning of the earthquake expecting their plans to be so ruthlessly interrupted, yet isn't this the same for all of us? Incidents can and do totally transform our lives. They can leave an indelible mark not just on individuals, but nations. Hagar's story is a perfect example.

The incident which altered Hagar's world was equally catastrophic and life-altering. God had told Abraham to go to a land that He would show him, the Promised Land, Canaan, one flowing with milk and honey, abundance and blessing, but later a famine had driven Abraham and his wife down to Egypt with disastrous consequences. Unquestionably Abraham got himself, his wife, Sarah, her maidservant, Hagar and the Egyptian Pharaoh into a real mess when he came bungling into Egypt with a false statement. Sarah was Abraham's half-sister and wife, but fearing he would be killed, he asked his wife to tell a lie and tell Pharaoh she was his sister. 'Please say you are my sister, that it may be well with me for your sake, and that I may live because of you' (Genesis 12:13, NKJV). It caused him, Sarah and Hagar to be thrown out of Egypt and, instead of becoming a blessing, Abraham must have been considered the opposite, given what transpired after he and Sarah arrived there – 'great plagues' because of the lie (Genesis 12:17, NKJV). Solomon wrote: 'Whoso keepeth his mouth and his tongue keepeth his soul from troubles' (Proverbs 21:23).

How accurate this has proved since, for great trouble has stalked Abraham's seed from that day forward. Of course, God blessed and protected Abraham and Sarah, even in Egypt. God is a faithful God! But, as we shall discover, because of one careless and untrue statement, Abraham still came away from Egypt with an embarrassing rebuke from a pagan king.

The full extent of the harm Abraham caused is only revealed much later when the slave girl Hagar – whom he and Sarah received in Egypt – became a great source of anxiety to him and his family.

Talk about an incident which changed their world and a gift that completely backfired!

For further thought, prayer and reflection

- Has an incident in your life changed everything?
- How have you reacted to this change – positively or negatively?
- What was the single incident which changed the status and life of Hagar when she was in Egypt?
- Name characters in the Bible whose lives were changed by sudden incidents.
- Name some incidents in history which have changed the world as we know it.
- Has 911 and other atrocities by Islamic terrorists given rise to prejudice within your own heart against Muslims? If so, ask God to forgive this and replace the feeling with love, forgiveness and compassion.
- What was the incident involving Abraham which dramatically changed Hagar's situation?

Note

1. J.K. Rowling, *The Guardian* newspaper, Sunday 11/1/15.

Three:
The Power of the Tongue

The human voice is the most beautiful instrument of all, but it is the most difficult to play.
(Richard Strauss)[1]

When it comes to spectacular fallout following a wrong choice of words, the name of Abraham is one of the first to spring to mind. Rash statements, inappropriate and untruthful remarks repeatedly bring unwelcome consequences, and all of us have been guilty of such folly.

Abraham may have lived thousands of years ago but he, too, was no exception to opening his mouth and saying the wrong thing at the wrong time. Just one loose comment by the great patriarch, the words, 'She is my sister' (Genesis 12:19, NKJV) cost Abraham, Sarah, Hagar and so many others, dearly. It may not sound like such a bad sentence, but it wasn't true, of course, and that's what caused all the fuss.

Such words are often used during moments of anger, fear,

insensitivity, quarrelling or pride, or when we're stressed and not thinking straight. Sadly, these words almost always cause regrettable incidents in our lives. How often, for example, have we said to ourselves, 'I really put my foot in it that time!'?

Despite the hardship of the famine back in Abraham's own country, the fact is, he wasn't told by God to go to Egypt and, consequently, the results were disastrous. His actions and his words when he first arrived in Egypt appear so inconsistent with his normally flawless walk with God – particularly his words. Abraham was a man clearly out of his comfort zone, and frankly, out of his depth.

Abraham had moved to a foreign country where he assumed things would be easier, more prosperous and where he could feed his family – something which is perfectly normal, of course – except God hadn't called Abraham to Egypt, but to Canaan.

Abraham is like most of us. He found it easier to trust God for the future than the present. And so he did his own thing. Understandably he was fed up with famine and so he entered a fantasy world where he assumed he and Sarah could exist without complications. God was with him and everything would work out in the end, no matter where he chose to live.

This is not necessarily true! God has a purpose and a plan for all of us – and this includes the geographical location we reside in. God told Abraham to go to Canaan, not Egypt, and when he disobeyed this command, difficulty soon emerged.

Other than Jesus Christ, of course, Abraham is unquestionably one of the greatest men to have ever lived in human history. Even today, Jews, Muslims and Christians all look to Abraham as their patriarch and God called him 'friend' (James 2:23); yet isn't it comforting to know that Abraham was still capable of putting his foot in it?

Abraham was regarded as a great man of God, not a perfect man, of course, but a righteous man nonetheless; a man who continually built altars of sacrifice to God wherever he went.

Telling blatant lies, therefore, to the pharaoh would not have sat well on Abraham's Christian CV. The immensity of this deception meant that Abraham's spiritual reputation would have been considerably damaged.

Think of the wagging tongues at that time:

'Did you hear about the incident involving Abraham telling lies to the king?'

'I thought he was a man of God!'

'What a total hypocrite!'

True, his behaviour may not have been so godly, but let's not forget that Abraham was just a man. Religious people and even their leaders are frequently put on a pedestal and viewed as being without sin, yet the truth is, all are fallible, with the potential to be dishonest or mess up like everyone else.

In the case of Abraham, by concealing information from the King of Egypt that would have been customarily provided, he had put Pharaoh in a compromising situation, even though he was only trying to protect himself and his family. His motives may have been pure, but his methods left much to be desired. The Bible commentator Matthew Henry wrote: 'Crooked policy will not prosper. It brings ourselves and others into danger.'[2]

Instead of being a blessing, Abraham became a stumbling block to his neighbour. I'm sure Abraham must have kicked himself many times and repented much about his deceitful plan involving Pharaoh. Honesty is always the best policy; therefore Abraham would surely have thought to himself: 'If only I had told the truth!'

The regret experienced following a wrong comment doesn't

make things any easier, either, yet as the old saying goes: 'There's no point crying over spilt milk.' Often what's done is done – we can't unscramble eggs – but some mistakes are bigger than others and the consequences of Abraham's dealings may have haunted him for the rest of his life.

No wonder Solomon wrote: 'Death and life are in the power of the tongue: and they that love it shall eat the fruit thereof' (Proverbs 18:21). Solomon is saying that our words produce fruit – consequences – which can either be for good or for bad.

Abraham isn't the only person in life, of course, to create a problem over something he shouldn't have said. We've all been guilty of the same thing and it only reveals the sorry state of our own hearts. Jesus said: 'But what comes out of the mouth proceeds from the heart, and this defiles a person' (Matthew 15:18, ESV).

Quite often the words we speak outwardly expose who we really are inwardly. Our words reflect our hearts. The apostle Paul exhorts: 'Let your speech be always with grace, seasoned with salt, that ye may know how ye ought to answer every man' (Colossians 4:6).

In this world where degrading and harmful words are spoken over people's lives to pull them down and bring them under condemnation, and manipulate or rob individuals of their worth and ability, we can be a different voice, speaking affirming words that reflect the heart of God for a lost people without a shepherd, people needing His compassion. If our words are hurtful and even untrue, they have the power to destroy rather than restore. What seemed like such an innocent statement by Abraham – a little white lie – changed the course of many other people's lives, and with devastating consequences.

Renowned evangelist Billy Graham said:

The problems of the world could be solved overnight if men could get victory over their tongues. Suppose there was no anger, no profanity, no lying, no grumbling or complaining; suppose there were no dirty stories told, no unjust criticism – what a different world this would be! The Bible teaches that a man who can control his tongue can control his whole personality. We should ask ourselves three questions before we speak:

Is it true?

Is it kind?

Does it glorify Christ?

If we would always think before we speak, there would be much less evil speaking, and there would soon be a spiritual awakening that would sweep the church in America.[3]

In our age of social media such as Facebook, Twitter, Instagram and the Internet, everyone seems to want to say something, yet the reality is, not everyone has something useful to say. Wrong choice of words is all too common today. Social media is awash with some outrageous statements. Many of them are, admittedly, well-intentioned, but many are also damaging and reveal hearts which are clearly not seeking God's love.

Cyber bullying, for example, especially among young people, is a major problem today and the words people use are often negative, harmful and destructive. Young people have taken their own lives due to someone else using negative and condemning words. There is an old rhyme which goes: 'Sticks and stones may break my bones but words will never harm me', yet this is simply not true. Words do hurt and injure people and can be the cause of many broken relationships. The words we use matter! There is power in the tongue, and it can be used for either positive or negative reasons. As we read at the start of this chapter, the German composer Richard Strauss once said:

'The human voice is the most beautiful instrument of all, but it is the most difficult to play.'[4]

What choice of words do you use every day – positive or negative? Remember, 'Death and life are in the power of the tongue: and they that love it shall eat the fruit thereof' (Proverbs 18:21). Are you using the power God has given to you? Jesus said to His followers: 'Behold, I give you the authority to trample on serpents and scorpions, and over all the power of the enemy, and nothing shall by any means hurt you' (Luke 10:19, NKJV).

Consider some of the negative things we say:

I nearly died!

If he does that one more time I'm going to kill him!

That makes me sick!

There won't be many at the meeting tonight, they are all on holiday, and anyway, it's too wet!

Nothing good ever happens to me!

I'm one of the unluckiest people ever!

I couldn't win a raffle even if I was the only one who entered!

I'm too young! I'm too old! I'm not talented enough!

It's time to change our words because our words have influence and power.

Due to fear that he would lose his life, and the possible stress he was under regarding the famine, unusually Abraham chose to use negative words which not only impacted him but also his family and spoiled his godly witness.

The importance of using the right words is not just relative to our personal lives; it cannot be underestimated in terms of its significance in many public fields today, such as politics, broadcasting and in spiritual environments. As God's ambassadors, the voices we carry are crucial in either drawing people to God or driving those same people away.

Therefore, are our words uplifting, edifying, balanced, and even true? Are they gracious and kind? Paul exhorts us to 'Let no corrupt communication proceed out of your mouth, but that which is good to the use of edifying, that it may minister grace unto the hearers' (Ephesians 4:29).

Are the words we use kind, sweet and helpful to others? Or are they unkind, disparaging and destructive? The Bible highlights just how dangerous the tongue can be. The book of James says: 'And the tongue is a fire, a world of iniquity. The tongue is so set among our members that it defiles the whole body, and sets on fire the course of nature; and it is set on fire by hell' (James 3:6, NKJV).

James also adds: 'If anyone among you thinks he is religious, and does not bridle his tongue but deceives his own heart, this one's religion is useless' (James 1:26, NKJV).

Sadly there are too many 'religious ranters' in the Christian church today, and not just in pulpits. Facebook, Twitter and the Internet are awash with such people. They believe they are standing up for the gospel of truth and courageously speaking up for Jesus, yet the real truth is many of these albeit well-meaning people are presenting another gospel and another Jesus. Their arguments contradict the Word of God which seeks to restore and unify, not divide and conquer.

We hear constant debates about the importance of freedom of speech, and this is good because freedom of speech is a most important subject; nonetheless, freedom of speech is never a free-for-all – it necessitates responsibility. Words send messages and words produce consequences!

In an ever-increasing secular, and paradoxically, religious society, understandably many Christians feel the need to stand up for the faith and shout louder than before. In a world where it appears everyone else is to be heard and allowed a voice, but Christians are sometimes sidelined and ignored, having been considered no longer relevant, this impulse to 'speak up' is a perfectly normal response. There is understandable pressure on Christian leaders who believe it is their duty to stand up for the honour of the gospel. Why? Because as Bible-believing Christians, they do not believe that other religions are the way to God. Notwithstanding, it's essential Christians use the right language in order to properly influence others for God. Neither is it the duty of any Christian to attack other religions. The call of Christians is to 'preach the gospel' (Mark 16:15, NKJV), not their own fears, ignorance, politics or prejudices. The normally reliable Abraham, a man of prayer and passion for the things of God, uncharacteristically deviated away from preaching God's Word, and the results were life-changing. He spoke from his flesh and not from his spirit. Or, to use a well-known term – he chose to 'bend the truth'. In so doing it produced a change of circumstances which caused not only him, but Sarah and Hagar to endure a harsh new chapter in their lives.

As we go through life we get many opportunities to keep our mouth shut – perhaps we should take every one of them. When we don't, however, there's life after our verbal paroxysms and damaging assertions. No one is perfect, of course! Thankfully, there's mercy with God, with whom there is always a new beginning.

Still, the fear of living in a foreign country and being uprooted overnight must have terrified Hagar. Remember, she wasn't asked if she wanted to leave her homeland of Egypt. She wasn't given any 'familiarisation period' with her new family. She wasn't consulted as to whether or not she would like a change of career. She was simply told she was going, and that was all there was to it. Pharaoh didn't afford her a choice and neither did Abraham or Sarah.

A wrong choice of words by Abraham had ensured that. Hagar's world had changed for ever. The power of the tongue had produced a bittersweet fruit.

For further thought, prayer and reflection

- Are you quick to speak or slow to speak?
- Do you pray about the words you use or just say what you think or like?
- Do you use gracious and uplifting words – or are your words critical, cruel and condemning?
- Do you think before you speak in order to glorify Christ with your words?
- Have you considered speaking less and listening more?
- Are your words kind and gracious on social media sites and while communicating on the Internet?

Notes

1. izquotes.com.
2. christnotes.org.
3. Billy Graham, *Tame Your Tongue* (Bloomington, Indiana: Westbow Press – a division of Thomas Nelson and Zondervan).
4. izquotes.com.

Four:
End of an Era

You know that an end signals a new beginning, right?[1]

To paraphrase Andy Garcia – 'The end of an era is leaving the thing you cherish; a celebration of a culture you hold most dear.' Of course, the end of an era is not always regretted by people, especially if that same era contains unpleasant memories. If we're honest, there are periods in all of our lives which we are well and truly glad to see the back of – the conclusion of an unsatisfactory job, a difficult or abusive relationship, and escape from the school bully – none of the above things anyone would cherish.

Following years of oppression, the only thing Hagar probably cherished in Egypt was her familiarity and her reasonable level of security. Now she didn't even have that. To up sticks and move would have definitely been a frightening prospect for Hagar. The comparative comfort Abraham, Sarah and Hagar all enjoyed in Egypt was unexpectedly replaced by the uncertainty of the wilderness and the long, arduous and apprehensive journey which ultimately would end back in Canaan.

Overnight, this faithful Egyptian slave was denied the chance to say farewell to people who, no doubt, had been her friends and colleagues for many, many years. There was no time for a going-away party, no reminiscing about good times, no band playing and no send-off speeches. Things happened so fast poor Hagar probably didn't even have time to pack a case. For her, the end of an era had arrived, but not in the way she would ever have dreamed or even planned.

Think about it! One day Hagar was living in Egypt; the next day she was gone. One day she was surrounded by all of her friends and colleagues, and the next she was completely isolated. Talk about trauma and emotional strain! Talk about upheaval and uncertain times!

Having become Sarah's property, Hagar had no choice in the relocation matter. She immediately had to leave her homeland for good. Her time was up. Furthermore, because of Abraham's lies, the pharaoh had been left embarrassed, offended and angry. His pride was hurt and he wasn't in the mood to barter. The implications of all of this were immense for Hagar.

When Hagar's own 'end of an era' moment arrived unexpectedly, her life received a profound adjustment. There was no such thing as 'closure'. The world she'd known and understood for most of her life was turned upside down in an instant and would never be the same again. Hagar, of course, probably would have preferred to leave Egypt on good terms, giving notice, and knowing exactly where she was headed and what the future held, but that doesn't always happen – and neither is it necessarily God's plan for our lives.

Let's remember, Egypt had been Hagar's life; it was all she knew. She may not have liked the oppression, but it was home and what she was used to. Isn't it amazing how we learn to tolerate something we don't like? She may have resided in the servants' quarters, yet those living conditions were a palace compared to where she was going – to the Negev, Canaan, and to a land, a people and a culture she didn't understand; to a wilderness, no less!

Home would now become animal-skin tents with a wandering tribe whose language, culture and philosophy she didn't understand. The religion would have been vastly different to what she'd been used to in Egypt. The food would be dissimilar, too. The fashion would be unrecognisable compared with the custom of Egypt. She would be mingling with sheep, cattle, donkeys and camels. But let's imagine something else here. If a positive is to be found in Hagar's situation, perhaps the thought of leaving Egypt behind was a chance to evade the influence of Pharaoh and escape from a place she had grown tired of. After all, the end of something signals a new beginning, right?

Trapped inside an impregnable religious establishment, Hagar would have faced the same mundane tasks day after day. For years she might well have been trudging along in her daily occupation convinced things were as good as they were going to get. She must have asked herself many times 'Is this my lot in life?'; 'Am I destined to die in slavery in Egypt?'

The younger we are, of course, the more we tend to view the world through rose-tinted spectacles. We start out full of great anticipation, quest and invention. Such prospects appear endless to our youthful minds. The sky is the limit! Nothing can stop us achieving our goals and dreams. Then reality sets in and suddenly the world looks a very different place. This can be caused by the slave-like conditions many are forced to exist in – conditions just like Hagar endured. How would this monotony have left her feeling? What would it have meant to her confidence levels and self-esteem?

Are we stuck in a rut, in the past, or are we free to embrace the future?

Was this Hagar: Sick of a claustrophobic, controlling environment which seemed impossible to challenge and sick of long, exhausting hours which had wearied both her body and her soul? The end of an era had been screaming out to her, and now it was literally happening.

When our lives fly past like this, there's a constant awareness that time is scarce, and if we don't act quickly we will naturally fall far short of God's potential for our lives. I wonder, did Hagar feel the same way? Was she terrified of ending up unhappy and unfulfilled? Was she worried about the clock ticking and time running out? Was she anxious about missing the mark and not fulfilling her potential?

It's recorded that while the Bible gives us no record of Hagar's genealogy, legend has supplied her pedigree, as being the daughter of Pharaoh, the King of Egypt, the same who coveted the possession of Sarah in vain. This legendary source affirms that the Egyptian princess became so attached to Sarah that she told her royal father that she would accompany her when she returned to Abraham. 'What!' cried the king, 'thou wilt be no more than a handmaid to her!'

'Better to be a handmaid in the tents of Abraham than a princess in this palace', the daughter replied.[2]

These sentiments are similar to what David expressed when he said: 'For a day in Your courts is better than a thousand. I would rather be a doorkeeper in the house of my God Than dwell in the tents of wickedness' (Psalm 84:10, NKJV).

Whether Hagar truly yearned for such freedom no one knows,

but being a slave for so many years – firstly in Egypt and then in Canaan as Sarah's maidservant – it's likely she did dream of one day being set free, despite serving inside the most famous and opulent palace in the land. Certainly the legendary story seems to suggest this is so.

The reality of the journey she was about to embark upon, however, was hugely different to those far-reaching dreams. From the thriving commerce of Egypt and possibly a reputation as an accomplished slave, suddenly Hagar now found herself in a worse position when thrust into the rural life of a religious drifter and his wife. Becoming the servant and slave of a nomadic tribeswoman (Sarah) was not a great prospect. It would actually have been a step down for Hagar. Instead of 'promotion' it must have felt like a demotion. Yet she was leaving a nation that worshipped idols to one where she would find the true and living God. She was being lifted out of darkness into light, even though she wouldn't have recognised the hand of God upon her at this stage of her spiritual journey.

In the same way that Hagar's culture was altered overnight, church culture in the twenty-first century has also been revolutionised at lightning speed. While young people see church today as 'normal', there have been numerous changes which people of an older generation have struggled to adapt to. The entire language, ethos and philosophy of the church is so vastly different to what it has been in the past that if someone was raised from the dead and returned to their former church today, they would likely wonder what was going on!

Neither is this sweeping transformation in ecclesiastical circles due, solely, to the accessibility and increase of technology which, granted, has changed the way we 'do church' and function in society in general. The style of worship, how the message is delivered and how people dress in church today are all totally different to how we remember, if we have been around church a long time. In many churches or 'worship centres', as some are now referred to, hymn boards have been replaced by large TV screens and hymn books by choruses on PowerPoint.

Many of the traditional hymns have been dropped in favour of new contemporary music and in many churches the minister reads from iPad notes in preference to holding up an old King James Bible. The fervent, passionate and even 'hellfire and brimstone preaching' of the Puritan age has been exchanged for a gentler, shorter, more tactful and, in some cases, creative delivery. In many churches, video clips accompany the Word of God, and drama is used to help illustrate the preacher's message. I am not suggesting any of this change is negative; only that it is very different to how church was held in previous generations. Many assemblies have drastically changed the way they do things in their weekly meetings. Church services are today known as worship services. Song leaders are called worship leaders. We have more music, and a greater variety of music. The motive is good – so that we become more aware of our Creator and Saviour, Jesus Christ – and that we express worship in the words we sing and in the emotions that songs can convey. This is positive, but it is also immensely different to the conservative way services were presented in the past.

It should be no surprise, then, that some people find this radical change of church culture uncomfortable. People often become used to a traditional way of doing things, and can easily view a change in any area of their lives as an unnecessary interruption. While church has become a total culture shock for many, the irony is that the church today is a place people once only dreamed of being a part of. Church has progressed to the point where a fresh start has been made possible, a place where a different atmosphere exists and genuine opportunity to break free from all of the tried and tested religion of the past has become a reality; thus experiencing complete freedom to worship God. We often fear that which we don't understand, but this doesn't make it harmful.

Many people and churches are struggling to come to terms with what is clearly the end of an era, yet even in the face of great change, positive things can still emerge.

Just because God chooses to change the furniture doesn't mean the room is any less appealing.

Nevertheless, precipitous change, which ruthlessly forces us from one ethos to another or one culture to another, can be hard to adjust to, and great flexibility and adaptability is required if one is to survive. Many displaced people are experiencing this actuality today and it's not an easy readjustment.

History tells us that Hagar would have had a considerable amount of religion in her own life. In fact, archaeological evidence and excavated clay tablets show that people such as Hagar lived in a deeply religious society. The women in particular lived and breathed religion, because their lives were so closely connected with nature, on which they depended for survival. Belief in the gods/goddesses and in mythical stories was central to everything they did.

However, God would prove to Hagar that He is bigger, greater and more powerful than any one culture, denomination or religion – a fact she was about to discover. Ultimately, she would come to understand that no matter where we are, God can find us, fight for us and provide for us, and even shake us up!

Notwithstanding, leaving Egypt would still have been hard for Hagar. It was a makeover she couldn't ever have imagined – yet spiritually it was for her own good. She was going to live with one of God's chosen servants, the 'friend of God' (James 2:23, NKJV) Abraham and, more importantly, she was about to be exposed to the God of Abraham.

From a human perspective, she would not have understood this, but our plan is often a logical one, which doesn't allow for sudden change or the will of God. We have our destination all sorted, but God's plan is frequently illogical to our human understanding, a supernatural strategy beyond our comprehension. The Bible tells us: '"For my thoughts are not your thoughts, neither are your ways my ways," declares the LORD' (Isaiah 55:8, NIV 1984).

Hagar was about to experience this reality, but so, too, were Abraham, Sarah, Egypt – and the world. Hagar would be part of God's supernatural pattern, not only for her individual life, but for the nations regarding future generations. For her, things would never quite be the same again. There was a bigger spiritual picture at play. Leaving Egypt and ultimately moving to Canaan wasn't just about Hagar, or Abraham or Sarah – or even Pharaoh… individuals. It never is. God is on the throne and He is constantly orchestrating events in all of our lives. He is the conductor and we are the musicians.

While Hagar may have been shocked by her sudden departure from Egypt, God was not. As cruel and unjust as it may have appeared, Hagar's departure was pre-planned and part of something far bigger than her.

Like Queen Esther, who was called according to God's purpose for a specific task and time, Hagar's own path was being skilfully carved out by the design of Almighty God – a God who was working quietly in the background to a master plan – the building of not just one, but incredibly, two great nations.

For further thought, prayer and reflection

- How did Hagar's world change in terms of the culture she knew in Egypt and the new culture she had to accept?
- Have you experienced the end of an era in your personal life? How has this altered the environment you now live in?
- Have you experienced what is termed 'closure'? Were you able to say goodbye to that era and to those you were close to, or did you have to leave abruptly?
- If the answer to the above question is negative, how has this impacted your life?
- Are you tied to the past, or are you free to embrace a brand-new era?
- How has the culture of your church changed in recent years, and how has this made you feel?
- Have you been able to adjust to the modernity of church, or are you stubbornly resisting change making you resentful and even angry?
- Have you considered these changes may be for the best – in order to replace traditional religion with the liberty and freedom of Christ?

Notes

1. wittyprofiles.com.
2. https://www.biblegateway.com/resources/all-women-bible/Hagar.

Five:
Outside Looking In

The Bible is full of stories about how God's love is broad enough, deep enough, and high enough and long enough to draw in those who are treated as outsiders. Hagar's story is a poignant one.
(Anne Graham Lotz)[1]

I still recall how I suffered from an identity crisis during my early years in Eastern Europe, where I spent almost a decade. From the first day I arrived in Romania I felt like an outcast. This had nothing to do with the majority of Eastern Europeans, who were mostly welcoming, hospitable and friendly people; instead, my inferiority complex was due to experiencing a strange culture as well as having to exist in an environment I clearly wasn't prepared for. Arriving to live in Eastern Europe from the United Kingdom was never going to be easy.

I was tasked with learning a new language, gaining perspective on new religions, and I had to cope with driving on the opposite side of the road. Adjusting to unusual food wasn't straightforward either, while my dress code was initially far too formal. Thankfully, I eventually learned the 'do's' and 'don'ts' of my new culture and country, yet I always felt like a stranger. I suffered as an 'outsider'. I wasn't one of them. I had this constant sense of not fitting in; a feeling that never quite went away during my term in Eastern Europe.

How, then, did Hagar feel, leaving behind all of her friends and family as she departed from Egypt with Abraham and Sarah, setting out for a new country and a new life elsewhere. Did she initially experience that awful sense of not fitting in? Did she view herself as a total outsider? I am certain she did. The name Hagar means 'stranger', and being originally from Egypt she would never have been fully accepted into Abraham and Sarah's clan.

Hagar was an Egyptian by birth, so even though she ultimately became part of Abraham and Sarah's tribe following their less than inspiring exit from Egypt, she would have been considered an outsider and this would have caused her to feel much rejection. Unwelcome back in Egypt, she didn't fit in with her new people. Suddenly she belonged to no one!

Feeling like we're on the outside begins way back when we're young and trying desperately to impress friends and family members, and continues later in life when we are just as keen to belong to some social group. During our youth, we become skilled in pretending to fit in, talking about things we're not particularly interested in, and getting involved in preoccupations we don't necessarily enjoy. It's all part of trying to make ourselves appear 'normal'. Nevertheless, once we mature, there are still moments where the impression of not belonging anywhere or with anyone is all-consuming. This feeling occurs randomly, usually when we're in a group of people, whether they be friends, colleagues or family, who are having a good time. In the midst of laughter and conversation, suddenly we can become intensely aware of the truth: I don't fit in here.

Have you ever felt like you didn't fit in? It's a horrible reality and actually quite unsettling. Not feeling like we fit in isn't always a bad thing, however. If you don't feel you belong somewhere it's usually because you don't. Notwithstanding, most of the time we all like to have that sense of belonging and social compatibility. It's how God made us!

During those apprehensive early years with Abraham and Sarah, Hagar must have felt like a total misfit. No longer was she a relatively affluent slave within a prosperous environment. All of a sudden she was known as Hagar, the girl slave of Sarah, wife of Abraham, the man who had told lies to the King of Egypt. Knowing how people are, she wouldn't have been able to live this incident down quickly.

I wonder, was Hagar even more self-conscious and alienated because she was aware that every time Abraham looked at her his conscience was pricked? Did she sense that she was a constant reminder to Abraham of an incident and an event and a period in his otherwise godly life that had brought him and his household so much humiliation? What happened in Egypt may not have been Hagar's culpability, but mud sticks, and so great was Abraham's reputation, she would forever be associated with his deception and perhaps embarrassment.

Hagar had previously been a slave to a man (Pharaoh). Abandoned by him, she was now a slave to a woman (Sarah). She would just simply have to make the best of things. This change of circumstances must have brought with it both fear and trepidation as Hagar made that first journey into the wilderness away from everything she knew.

Such contrast Hagar would have undergone compared to her life back in Egypt! She and Abraham and Sarah were now very much on the outside. The future looked bleak and lonely. Every day Hagar would probably have been recounting life back in Egypt where she at least had some measure of family belonging and more lavish daily provision. She probably pined for former friends and family that were now well and truly part of her past.

Released in 2013, *The Butler* is an American historical drama, and tells the story of a young black man – Cecil Gaines (Forest Whitaker) – who, after leaving the South and finding employment at an elite hotel in Washington DC, gets the opportunity of a lifetime when he's hired as a butler at the White House. Over the course of the next three decades, Cecil has a front-row seat to the inner workings of the Oval Office, yet his life began in poverty, taking jobs wherever he could get them; then returning at night with nowhere to lay his head. This man was convinced that God never meant for anyone to be without a family.

Hagar, too, began to encounter life on the outside without family of her own; wandering in the wilderness with two people she couldn't relate to from a diverse culture and different spiritual background. It must have been a scary place! I have developed a special empathy for the Hagars of our modern world; the outsiders, if you like. I see them walking down the street every day, strangers who have moved to my own country of Northern Ireland from foreign shores seeking a better life and, like Hagar, not always feeling welcome. Many of them are precariously out of place and in need of assistance. My heart genuinely aches for them.

Today, when I meet foreign nationals in my own country, I see loneliness, fear and sadness written all over many of their faces. They often recoil and become recluse-like, affording little eye contact for fear of being racially abused or just unaccepted.

The incredible story of Jayne Olorunda illustrates the difficulties of having to face life on the outside, especially in Northern Ireland. Her story came to public attention when she wrote Legacy, published by Maverick House and lulu.com in December 2013 – an excellently written book about her experiences growing up in Northern Ireland. It documents the complications her family encountered with identity and the sometimes impossible realities of assimilation. Jayne was born and bred in Northern Ireland – a Catholic; she is probably among a small handful of people of colour who can say that in Ulster. It is sad that even now, in her thirties, black faces in Northern Ireland still stand out in the crowd. As such they have become targets to those elements in our society determined to keep their society white, those intent on living in bitterness. Jayne stated: 'I am Northern Irish, but I am also black and this is not a comfortable position to be in; at times it has felt like a disastrous combination.'

Jayne's father was originally from Nigeria and, intent on finding a better life, was offered a job in Belfast on his graduation, but everything changed for her family in 1980. On his way home from work, her dad stepped on a train that he would never step off. His fellow passengers included two IRA men who carried a bomb. The bomb exploded, obliterating Jayne's father and two others on the carriage. That bomb changed the face and experiences of her family forever. From there on she experienced life on the outside. Gone was financial stability, gone was their home, and worst of all, gone was their dad. The blast took him away along with any link they had to their Nigerian culture. From that day on, Jayne and her sisters became confused black girls in an all-white world. This incident, of course, made their fitting in even more difficult; Jayne's dad's death alienated them from Catholic communities, while their religion alienated them from Protestant communities. In short, they lacked identity at every level. Like Hagar, they felt as though they belonged to no one.

When people forgo a familiar environment and the friends and families they grew up with and try to fit into a new culture, life is tough enough, but when those same people face rejection, resulting in them feeling like outsiders, it can be incredibly daunting. Hagar would also have felt like an outsider, yet if anyone would have been able to relate to her apprehension, it would have been Abraham. He knew what it was like to separate from his own people and serve God in a land he was not familiar with so that God would make a great nation through him.

For example, prior to their experiences in Egypt, Abraham and Sarah began a journey that would direct them into unchartered spiritual territory. Leaving their homeland, they moved hundreds of miles south, to Canaan, a land flowing with the promises of God, yet void of the lifestyle they would have been used to. God had promised this land to Abraham and his offspring. From him would not only originate a family, tribe or clan, but an entire nation: Now the LORD said to Abram, 'Go forth from your country, And from your relatives And from your father's house, To the land which I will show you; And I will make you a great nation, And I will bless you, And make your name great; And so you shall be a blessing' (Genesis 12:1,2, NASB).

The purpose of God, therefore, isn't always that we live in the country of our birth, or stay in one job or in one church for a lifetime, although there is nothing wrong with this. Sometimes God wants us to step out of the boat and swim in the deep water; sometimes He does move us geographically in order to move us on spiritually. Sometimes He does allow us to sample life on the periphery.

Significantly, years after her own departure from Egypt, the Almighty spoke to Hagar in a similar way to how He'd spoken to Abraham, promising to create a great nation through her son, Ishmael. There was a purpose and plan even in her wilderness experiences and even though she dwelt in a foreign land God's hand was on her. 'And as for Ishmael, I have heard you. Behold, I have blessed him, and will make him fruitful, and will multiply him exceedingly. He shall beget twelve princes, and I will make him a great nation' (Genesis 17:20, NKJV).

Perhaps, like Hagar, you've been left languishing on the outside of the country of your birth, separated from people you grew up with, and you can't understand this. Maybe you've found yourself on the outside of a church you belonged to for years, or you've just retried from life-time employment or experienced the end of a long-term relationship. Maybe you've been excluded by a group of friends you didn't fit in with, or have suffered the terrible aftershocks of an incident which has dramatically reshaped your life. This has left you on the outside, looking in and feeling hurt, disappointed and even disorientated. Nonetheless, it's during these spells we can discover the purpose of God for our lives and how incredibly real God is. Often, in those dark, lonely times, God draws especially near and becomes the faithful friend we require.

Maybe you haven't been able to take any more and have

deliberately isolated yourself. You ran to the edge in order to avoid the pain of your present circumstances. The good news is God loves you and, even when you feel you can't continue, He's waiting for you on the outside of your journey. God has promised never to abandon us. When times are hard, lonely and uncertain; when we feel like outsiders, God is nearer than we realise – He's a constant 'friend who sticks closer than a brother' (Proverbs 18:24, NKJV).

Today there are millions of disappointed, displaced and distressed people like Hagar, people who see themselves as being on the outside, yet God is always present and moved by their circumstances. Are you one of them? Are you fearful for the future? Are you frightened and certain God is gone?

God hasn't buried you, He has planted you. He's isolated you in a dark place for your development and according to His great purpose.

As Hagar trooped through the wilderness, and feeling like she belonged to no one, God was right there beside her. All along a loving and compassionate God was ordering her steps and drawing her closer to Himself. When Hagar was awake, God was watching out for her, and when she slept, the same God was observing her situation. Regardless of her dramatically changing circumstances, God's plan was taking shape in her life.

While Hagar was focused on the outside, God was doing a work on the inside.

In her own pain, and in God's time, Hagar, like the psalmist, would discover that "God is our refuge and strength, A very present help in a time of trouble' (Psalm 46:1, NKJV).

She may not yet have believed in the true and living God, but the true and living God never stopped believing in her.

For further thought, prayer and reflection

- Do you feel like you don't fit in?
- Were you a good mixer when you were young or did you often feel on the outside?
- Are you a foreigner trying to adapt to a new country? How is this experience affecting you?
- What can be done to make foreigners feel more at home in your country?
- Have you considered that God has moved you geographically to get your attention?
- How aware of others are you that they may be feeling left on the outside?

Note

1. Anne Graham Lotz, *Wounded by God's People* (London: Hodder & Stoughton, 2013).

Six:
Too Early for Spring

Patience gets a workout when God's answer is no answer. In other words, God's answer is not always yes or no; sometimes He says, 'Not now!'
(T.D. Jakes)[1]

One February evening in 2015, I was thrilled to see the sun splitting the trees and the temperature unusually high for my daily walk. A short time after setting off on my trek, I excitedly exclaimed to a passing jogger, 'Is it too early for spring?'

'You can't fit February into May,' he replied. I was just about to discover how true that statement was. I began to notice the sky becoming black and the wind picking up considerably. I'd chosen to wear fewer clothes than normal due to how spring-like it was when I'd parked my car earlier, but I should have known not to trust Irish conditions – especially in the month of February! A storm was coming and I was a long way from my finishing point. Sleet and snow duly arrived, the heavens opened and I got totally drenched.

Less than an hour earlier I'd convinced myself it was spring, but the elements soon reminded me how it was mid-winter. I'd tried to fit February into May, but it didn't work – and why would it? Nevertheless, have you noticed how every day many of us try to fit February into May?

What am I saying? Sometimes we will go to extraordinary lengths in order to gain possessions and obtain things we covet, even though the time isn't right to receive them. If we're honest, all of us tend to gravitate towards things long before we're meant to have them. How many people, for example, have charged into a new job, a ministry, a marriage, a business venture, or started a family, knowing deep down it wasn't the right time, but desperate to have it anyway?

The good news is: God does not want to withhold good things from us, for He has an appointed time to make them available. Habakkuk wrote: 'For the vision is yet for an appointed time, but at the end it shall speak, and not lie: though it tarry, wait for it; because it will surely come, it will not tarry' (Habakkuk 2:3).

Abraham and Sarah tried to 'shift the seasons' by fast-forwarding the birth of Isaac, but you can't make right what's wrong. Ishmael came instead – his birth due to the impatience of Sarah and Abraham, who rejected God's time schedule regarding the promised son. This experienced godly couple ignored the words of Solomon, who said: 'To every thing there is a season, and a time to every purpose under the heaven' (Ecclesiastes 3:1).

To be fair, it was Sarah, not Abraham, who subtly and skilfully created a situation which she thought would speed things up, but the consequences were still devastating.

In God's divine purpose, Isaac's birth – he would be the promised son – was still some years away; so, she took matters into her own hands when she asked her husband to sleep with Hagar, their maidservant. Sarah was more than likely beginning to panic about her barren situation. Like other biblical superwomen – Rebekah, Rachel, Hannah – Sarah was unable to give birth naturally at this point in her life. The couple had dreamed of a son, but where was he?

So Sarah came up with a creative idea – a logical one that allowed for her passing years – the idea of a surrogate mother. The Bible says: 'Now Sarai Abram's wife bare him no children: and she had an handmaid, an Egyptian, whose name was Hagar. And Sarai said unto Abram, Behold now, the LORD hath restrained me from bearing: I pray thee, go in unto my maid; it may be that I may obtain children by her. And Abram hearkened to the voice of Sarai. And Sarai Abram's wife took Hagar her maid the Egyptian, after Abram had dwelt ten years in the land of Canaan, and gave her to her husband Abram to be his wife. And he went in unto Hagar, and she conceived' (Genesis 16:1–4).

Just like today, of course, this procedure is packed with conceivable conflict. This seemed like such an obvious solution. Sarah just wanted to erase the embarrassment of not being able to give birth which, in the culture of her day, brought with it a certain stigma, while Abraham longed for his successor to arrive – a son he could instruct and train in the things of God.

For years this couple had seen no progress in relation to the birth of a son, leaving them at breaking point. Hagar was living in the midst of this atmosphere and, who knows, maybe even encouraging them both not to give up, yet as often happens when we don't hear from God in our own timeframe, we decide to give Him a helping hand, even though God doesn't require our help. This is what Sarah chose to do and, as we shall discover, the consequences were awful.

This impatience not only caused major problems in their home, it also fashioned far wider implications for our world today. For example, from a global point of view, Ishmael's descendants are in constant conflict with Abraham's children through Isaac, but significantly are also in constant conflict amongst themselves. The Bible prophesied that, in relation to Ishmael, who is regarded as the forefather of the Islamic faith, 'His hand shall be against every man' (Genesis 16:12, NKJV). Many recognise this hostility today in the shape of Islamic extremists persecuting Christians and people of other faiths – and lots of Bible scholars agree this feud all began with an impetuous decision by Sarah and Abraham not to wait on the son of promise. The psalmist wrote, 'As for God, his way is perfect: the word of the LORD is tried: he is a buckler to all those that trust in him' (Psalm 18:30).

Rather than wait on God for the right door of opportunity, Abraham and Sarah created their own door and painted it in God's colours. It was too early for spring, but they tried to fit February into May anyway!

This part of Abraham and Sarah's story is not unfamiliar to the modern world, for the reality is barrenness is no stranger to the twenty-first century. Numerous couples struggle with fertility. Not all women succeed in getting pregnant, while others choose to adopt. Then there are those who opt for a child to be birthed by a surrogate mother.

In the case of Abraham and Sarah, however, the child of promise was already planned by God – he would be born later – the problem was, neither Abraham or Sarah were prepared to wait for this day. But God's calendar was vastly different to theirs.

The writer of Ecclesiastes thought to be Solomon says: 'He has made everything beautiful in its time' (Ecclesiastes 3:11, NKJV). Thousands of years ago, Isaiah also wrote: 'But those who wait on the LORD Shall renew their strength; They shall mount up with wings like eagles, They shall run and not be weary, They shall walk and not faint' (Isaiah 40:31, NKJV).

Probably the best known story of patience in the Bible is found in the life of Job. To prove Job's faithfulness to the Lord, God allowed the devil to destroy everything Job owned.

Job was a wealthy man, until he lost his livestock and servants, even his children. However, Job did not blame God. He accepted that God had a plan and would be patient for God to reveal His plan. Waiting on God during lean times is one of the hardest parts of the Christian life, but if that is you, be encouraged because even the great Abraham and Sarah struggled in this area.

Abraham had no heir and that was a major problem for a man with such a massive spiritual reputation in Israel. But Sarah had a maidservant and she said to Abraham, 'Go and sleep with her.' This wasn't a question for discussion. The couple didn't pray about it or wait to see if it was appropriate. Abraham and Sarah's patience had run out, yet if we're honest, patience is regularly abandoned by all of us. Filling that 'all-important slot' or 'getting the job done' becomes more of a priority than waiting on a better solution from God Himself.

How many businesses, political parties and churches have failed, not because of lack of effort or genuinely good intentions, but due to impulsive decisions which didn't have to be made?

The apostle James wrote, 'But let patience have her perfect work, that ye may be perfect and entire, wanting nothing' (James 1:4). While the writer to the Hebrews commented, 'For ye have need of patience, that, after ye have done the will of God, ye might receive the promise' (Hebrews 10:36).

When Joseph's brothers sold him as a slave, he didn't understand all that was happening, but he trusted God to work out His plan in His time. Joseph patiently worked faithfully in each situation he was in. He waited for God to fulfil His promise that Joseph would be a leader of his people (Genesis 37:5–11). He had to be patient as he waited on God, but how many times did he also wonder why he was sitting in a prison cell? God, though, eventually elevated Joseph to great power and responsibility. Not only was he a leader of his people, but he ruled over the people of Egypt too. But patience was needed to allow God to accomplish His purposes in the life of Joseph and his family.

Luke chapter 2 tells the story of the birth of Christ. The Holy Ghost had revealed to a man named Simeon that he would not see death until he had seen the birth of the Messiah. The Bible does not indicate how long Simeon had waited for the birth of Christ, but the fact that it says he would not die until he saw the Saviour indicates that he had waited some time.

After Jesus arrived in the temple, Simeon was led by the Spirit to visit Him there. Simeon took Jesus in his arms and thanked God that the promised child had arrived. Joseph and Mary were surprised by Simeon's actions. Simeon, though, knew otherwise and that he could now finally depart in peace.

As we read above, T.D. Jakes said:

'Patience gets a workout when God's answer is no answer. In other words, God's answer is not always yes or, no; sometimes He says, "Not now!"'[2]

God's 'no' is not a rejection; it's often just a redirection! I must confess patience isn't one of my strongest points. I'm not saying I want everything to happen today, but it would be nice!

In the Old Testament there's a powerful story of how the mighty prophet Samuel, along with David's father, Jesse, were found wanting when it came to 'waiting on God' for the right man at the right time. God's chosen man to succeed Saul was David. In fact, those whom Samuel and Jesse initially considered anointed and appropriate replacements for Saul were not anointed at all.

After God spoke to Samuel and sent him to Jesse's house to find Saul's successor, Samuel chose a man called Eliab. So certain was Samuel that he had found 'God's man' he declared, 'Surely the LORD's anointed is before [me]' (1 Samuel 16:6). But God rebuked him, saying, 'Look not on his countenance, or on the height of his stature; because I have refused him: for the LORD seeth not as man seeth; for man looketh on the outward appearance, but the LORD looketh on the heart' (1 Samuel 16:7).

In other words, God was giving Samuel a most important lesson in his life; namely, there is a difference between the choices which are made in the 'flesh' and the choices which are birthed in the 'spirit'. What we see with our physical eyes is not always what God is doing in the spirit.

David was far from perfect himself, of course; his sins relating to Uriah and Bathsheba, when he committed adultery with Bathsheba and murdered Uriah, are proof of this, but God's timing and choice was perfect.

Maybe you are waiting on God answering your prayers. You've been waiting for what seems like an eternity for something, but it still hasn't arrived.

Ladies: perhaps you are waiting for 'Mr Right', or your desire is to have a child and family.

Gentlemen: Maybe you have been promised promotion at work, a better salary and a better position at the local sports' club or an interesting role at the church you belong to.

Perhaps you have been praying for a loved one and that person is still indifferent towards God. Maybe you've been praying about one of your rebellious children. Whatever the situation, there is no timing like God's timing.

Don't settle for second best. Don't be tempted to sell yourself short of what God has purposed for you. Don't invent your own solution like Sarah did. It only leads to disillusionment and in many cases, painful experiences. Pray through and keep in mind the words of Jeremiah when he declared: 'For I know the thoughts that I think toward you, saith the LORD, thoughts of peace, and not of evil, to give you an expected end' (Jeremiah 29:11).

God has great plans for you, but in His time. Of course, it's hard to understand why God doesn't allow these things to happen immediately. But God works everything out when He is ready, not when we are ready.

The astounding thing about the birth of Isaac was God had promised it to both Abraham and Sarah years previously, and He delivered what He promised. The Bible states: 'For Sarah conceived, and bare Abraham a son in his old age, at the set time of which God had spoken to him' (Genesis 21:2).

He had purposed a time and a season for it all along; problem was, like most of us, Abraham and Sarah couldn't wait for such a day. Abraham and Sarah couldn't wait for Isaac, they couldn't wait for God's best, and they couldn't wait for spring. They wanted Ishmael, instead. If both had been able to wait, the very child they dreamed of was on the way all the time. Failure to wait brought immense problems later on, but this wasn't the only reason they experienced heartache, however. Something else was provoking them and festering in the background, something much more deadly and disruptive, and something which is causing much heartache in our world today – the toxic emotion of anger.

For further thought, prayer and reflection

• Have you ever tried to fit February into May?

• Have you ever rushed into something which later came back to haunt you?

• How patient are you in relation to waiting on the promises of God?

• Do you believe that God will keep His promise to you in His time?

• What mistake did Abraham and Sarah make when exercising their own impatience?

• Name some Bible characters who were patient regarding the promises of God.

• If God still hasn't answered your prayers, are you considering intervening to make something happen, or are you prepared to wait for God's best?

Notes

1. mobile.twitter.com.
2. mobile.twitter.com.

Seven:
The Consequences of Anger

Angry people are not always wise.
(Jane Austen, Pride and Prejudice)[1]

Some time ago I felt the wrath of someone I'd deeply hurt – a person I'd known and respected for years. Though I never intended to upset this individual, it was clear he was indignant and he let me know by his ruthless response. Those actions of retaliation were so heartless I was left shocked, and guess what? I, too, became hurt and angry. Instead of dealing with the situation and walking away, I made the mistake of reacting in anger myself; instead of allowing the situation to calm down, I responded in the wrong way – something I will always regret.

I don't normally respond to provocation with more provocation, but on this occasion my emotions simply got the better of me. All of a sudden two people were now hurt, two people were at war, and friends who once shared great fellowship and harmony became estranged from one another. While all of the anger finally subsided, of course, sadly the relationship was never quite the same afterwards. Anger has a way of destroying things.

Underneath anger there's hurt, usually because underneath hurt, there's previously been great love and mutual respect. This may have been the case when Sarah and Hagar clashed over the impending birth of Ishmael. It is not only hate that creates conflict. So, too, does love. This is manifestly illustrated, not only in the lives of Isaac and Ishmael, but also in the lives of other biblical characters in the book of Genesis such as Jacob and Esau, Leah and Rachel, Joseph and his brothers. Love unites and love divides.

The two women had lived together in Canaan for many years and, prior to the conception of Ishmael, they probably got on quite well. The longevity of Hagar's stay in the house is certainly evidence of this. Hagar had lived with Abraham and Sarah for at least ten years before the birth of Ishmael and didn't leave until the boy became a teenager. Indeed, Sarah and Abraham probably grew to deeply love and respect their maidservant Hagar during this time.

Sarah's love for Abraham undoubtedly collided with Hagar's situation in carrying Abraham's child. While things may not have been perfect, more than likely a mutually respectful relationship existed between them. That all changed during Hagar's pregnancy, however, when the animosity between the two women resulted in Hagar twice having to leave the household before the entire conflict concluded.

The first sign of a breakdown in their relationship happened when Sarah became increasingly insecure and angry at the thought of Hagar carrying Abraham's baby. She had become extremely displeased, having sensed Hagar's own raised status within the home, due to the fact that she was now the one ready to deliver Abraham's dream child.

Naturally, fireworks flared between the two women, and this seems to have resulted in Sarah finding a way to mistreat Hagar, who she blamed for all her troubles. Angry people often require a scapegoat, and that person is frequently one of their closest colleagues. The Hebrew text uses a significant word to describe Sarah's treatment of Sarah. She 'afflicted' her. This is the same word which would later be employed to describe how the Egyptians 'afflicted' the Israelites in the book of Exodus. Given that Hagar was herself an Egyptian, we see in Sarah's mistreatment of Hagar almost a hint of revenge. It demonstrates that even people claiming to have the Spirit of God can sometimes still be quite vindictive and unforgiving. Unable to deal with her own anger at Hagar's pregnancy, Sarah approached her husband Abraham with her complaint. The Bible records: 'And Sarai said unto Abram, My wrong be upon thee: I have given my maid into thy bosom; and when she saw that she had conceived, I was despised in her eyes: the LORD judge between me and thee. But Abram said unto Sarai, Behold, thy maid is in thine hand; do to her as it pleaseth thee. And when Sarai dealt hardly with her, she fled from her face' (Genesis 16:5–6).

Spare a thought for Hagar! She had gone from the oppression and slavery of Egypt, to experiencing the disorder and disunity and consummate anger of a so-called godly home in Canaan – and only because she did what she'd been asked to do.

This suggests to us how church may not be a perfect place, and neither are spiritual people and their homes. We should be willing to extend grace to other believers. Christians are subject to the same difficulties in life as everyone else, the same domestic disputes and unrest, the same problems, fears and anxieties. Abraham and Sarah were no different. Clearly all was not well in

Abraham and Sarah's abode, yet that didn't mean that God wasn't there. True, there would have been daily prayer at the usual altars and praise ascending to God. Hagar would undoubtedly have noticed the difference in Abraham's daily life and the life of Pharaoh and his religious companions back in Egypt, yet the longer things went on without the arrival of a child the more anger brewed below the surface. This would probably have expressed itself in frequent outbursts and 'temper tantrums' by Sarah and possibly by Abraham, too. What was once a house of peace may well have become a house of strife and contention!

One can always tell when anger is present – there's an uneasy atmosphere. It's as though someone or something is ready to explode at any moment. That's not to say there was no love in Abraham's home, but the fact that he and Sarah had no children had become a major stumbling block to the pair of them. It had become a most important issue, the only show in town. Add to this the fact that of all people, an Egyptian slave girl was now carrying Abraham's child! This would have caused daily frustration evidenced by the mean manner in which Sarah retaliated against Hagar who may not have been blameless either, by the way – in fact, the Bible states that after becoming pregnant with Ishmael, Hagar 'no longer respected her mistress' (Genesis 16:4, CEB). Nothing like a little bit of promotion to swell someone's head!

Hagar's sudden, prominent status may have led to an arrogance and pride which provoked the strife and dissension within the home. Sarah had created the monster, and Hagar responded by perhaps flaunting her new-found status over her mistress – not the brightest idea for a young foreigner battling against a woman desperate for her husband's approval!

As the bearer of Abraham's child, Hagar is clearly not happy to be considered a servant any longer. For example, I wonder, did Hagar begin to taunt Sarah, causing her to despise her maidservant. Did she begin to feel superior to Sarah? Perhaps Hagar sensed promotion in the home and let Sarah know about it.

Ann Graham Lotz wrote in *Wounded by God's People:*

As the one who now carried Abraham's baby, Hagar's position in the household must have been greatly elevated. But then…! Did she come to the startling conclusion that she, not Sarah, would be the one to give this great man the thing he had always dreamed of … a son? The thought must have exploded in her mind … Oh, my goodness. I'm carrying the Child of promise! Did it begin to occur to her that she now had exceptional value in the household? Value that she could barter for better treatment. A more exalted position. A more luxurious tent. Servants of her own. Did her Egyptian upbringing surface in her attitude as she became arrogant and self-centred? Did her tone of voice drip with condescension when she spoke to Sarah? Did she raise her eyebrows, look down her nose, toss her hair and dismiss her mistress as an inferior nuisance? Was she no longer quick to serve, but slow and resentful at being asked to do anything?[2]

They say: 'Hell hath no fury like a woman scorned!' This was Sarah. Angry at being barren and then having to cope with Hagar being pregnant produced a variety of emotions which would have affected her physically, spiritually, and even relationally.

Anger carries a price tag, and if not handled properly results in actions we later regret. Anger is a normal, healthy emotion, but managing it can be a problem for many people who find it difficult to keep their anger under control. Anger is raging all over the world. The recent atrocities in the Middle East, and in many other regions, are proof of this. The world is sick and full of hatred as people become less and less compassionate. Many people don't even realise how angry they are; which, I suppose, is the most worrying development of all! Switch on any daily news broadcast on radio, TV or the Internet, and what do you see?

A total disregard for human life caused by underlying anger.

Groups, with political and religious objectives, are carrying out the most heinous crimes, and at the very root of their violent actions are not necessarily ideology or any particular cause; instead it's unrestrained anger. This is concerning because anger in the heart will eventually lead to violence on the streets and ultimately conflict.

Sitting in a coffee shop one morning I was touched by the words of a young girl who'd arrived at the booth beside me to begin a business meeting with two male colleagues. Breezing into the shop, she placed her bag down on the table and announced: 'Good morning, my beautiful little fellow human beings, how are we all doing this morning?'

This girl was vividly cheery and clearly spirited, loving and interested in people; people she described explicitly as her 'beautiful little fellow human beings'. As I sat opposite, this refreshing approach spoke to my heart. It triggered an interesting thought within me.

Do we love or hate our fellow human beings? Are we glad to see one another, or do we detest the sight of one another, and even desire to destroy one another? Are our fellow human beings friends or strangers, brothers or enemies? Are they beautiful or horrible? Are we angry with people, or do we cut them some slack?

Of all the things in the human heart, anger can be one of the most intense, destructive, and unhealthy emotions that we can experience. If not handled in the proper way, it can have drastic life-changing consequences. Anger may be caused by pressures of work, family, or even from being the innocent victim of another's wrongdoing. Left unresolved, anger creates an intense desire to destroy something. Regardless of the reason for anger, the Bible has answers on what causes it, examples of righteous anger and unrighteous anger, and how we should deal with it. Not all anger is wrong. The Bible says: "'Be angry, and do not sin": do not let the sun go down on your wrath, nor give place to the devil' (Ephesians 4:26–27, NKJV).

Anger is not the fruit of righteousness and peace. James the apostle wrote, 'Know this, my beloved brothers: let every person be quick to hear, slow to speak, slow to anger; for the anger of man does not produce the righteousness of God' (James 1:10, ESV). There are professing Christians who flaunt their anger as evidence of so-called authority. The truth is, however, all they are really doing is revealing just how ungodly they are.

Sarah's earlier decision to appoint Hagar as the means by which both she and Abraham could produce the son of promise now appeared distinctly flawed and, not surprisingly, raw anger emerged; yet I wonder how this display of anger by Sarah impacted Hagar? How did it fit with Abraham and Sarah's beliefs? Would it have put Hagar off the God of Abraham? It certainly wasn't representative of the God of peace and love Abraham and Sarah professed to follow.

Experts believe there are many forms of anger which include annoyance, touchiness or animosity. When we react to criticism, threat or frustration, we may become angry – and this is mostly a healthy reaction. Anger has also been defined as a secondary response to feeling sad, lonely, insecure or frightened. But when anger becomes a full-blown rage, our judgement and thinking can become impaired and we are more likely to do and say unreasonable and irrational things. Today anger management courses help people deal with their anger.

Ambrose Bierce wrote: 'Speak when you are angry and you will make the best speech you will ever regret.'[3]

Anger usually means we've been hurt. Hurt results in us lashing out at the person we believe hurt us and, let's be honest, lashing out rarely leads to a happy conclusion.

Moses may have been regarded as a mighty man of God, yet he was forbidden by Him to enter the Promised Land. Striking a rock in temper cost Moses his lifelong desire to lead Israel into the Promised Land – an honour given to his successor Joshua instead!

Doesn't this prove how seriously God treats anger?

Many health issues linked to unresolved anger include high blood pressure, heart attack, depression, anxiety, colds, flu, and problems with digestion. Anger results from jealousy and unforgiveness issues. Anger is a universal problem. It's been said: 'Holding on to anger is like drinking poison and expecting the other person to die.'[4]

Anger is not limited to one age group, culture, race, economic level, social status, educational background, or any other classification. Unresolved anger is one of the chief contributing factors to the destruction of marriages, the breakdown of families, and the weakening of both secular and religious communities.

Paul wrote: 'But now you must put them all away: anger, wrath, malice, slander, and obscene talk from your mouth … Put on then, as God's chosen ones, holy and beloved, compassionate hearts, kindness, humility, meekness, and patience, bearing with one another and, if one has a complaint against another, forgiving each other; as the Lord has forgiven you, so you also must forgive' (Colossians 3:8,12–13, ESV).

People recoil and retreat from all forms of intolerance, anger, bitterness and hatred, and this was Hagar. She just couldn't take any more. She'd had enough of the nasty atmosphere and the abusive comments from her mistress. She was tired of tip toeing around the place; of feeling her stomach churn with nerves every time Sarah entered the room. These people were saying one thing and doing another. It was wrong and hypocritical and was now having a negative influence upon her. She was fed up, too, with the threat of eviction from her home and the general fear-factor being administered by the cruel Sarah. True, she was carrying Abraham's child, but wasn't that what Sarah wanted? Why would she treat Hagar so badly?

If she couldn't retaliate, then what else could Hagar do? She was left with no other choice – a drastic decision, yes, but the only choice remaining – to pack her things and run, run… run away!

For further thought, prayer and reflection

- What made Sarah so angry?
- Are you feeling angry with yourself or with others? Has this anger spilled over to cause problems in your personal and private life?
- How is the presence of anger influencing your life? If you find anger is dominating your life and ruining your relationships, it might be time to consider taking an anger management course.

Notes

1. Jane Austen, *Pride and Prejudice*, goodreads.com.
2. Anne Graham Lotz, *Wounded by God's People* (London: Hodder &

Stoughton, 2013), pp. 58,59.

3. goodreads.com.

4. goodreads.com.

Eight:
Standing Up or Standing Out

*Darkness cannot drive out darkness; only light can do that. Hate
cannot drive out hate; only love can do that. Hate multiplies hate.
Violence multiplies violence, and toughness multiplies toughness.*
Martin Luther King Jr.[1]

Sarah's mistreatment of her maidservant must have been quite
ferocious. After all, why would a pregnant mother like Hagar
choose to flee into the wilderness all alone? It would be like
writing your own death warrant. How did she expect to survive?
She'd clearly reached a point, of course, where she couldn't take
anymore harassment or humiliation and, when we reach such a
stage, we don't always think rationally. Decisions are often made
from our hearts, not our heads. How many days, weeks or even
months had this ill-treatment of Hagar by Sarah lasted? Had
Sarah deliberately and cunningly been trying to drive her rival
out of the house for some time, using unscrupulous and devious
methods? Did Sarah withdraw Hagar's normal privileges? Did

she make promises and fail to keep them? Was her aim to break Hagar's resolve and spirit, thus getting her to quit her post? Jealousy and insecurity can make people stoop to such wicked measures and Sarah may well have been no exception. Neither can we judge Hagar for refusing to take anymore.

Only after we have walked a mile in the shoes of others who have suffered constant intimidation can we begin to understand what they've gone through. Hagar was tired of being made to feel like a second-class citizen by her mistress Sarah. Having witnessed oppression for so many years while in Egypt, Hagar was now experiencing bullying in Canaan – a place she probably didn't expect to find it. The daily undermining by Sarah became too much for Hagar so, one day, she simply downed tools and announced, 'You know what, I'm out of here!' In other words she took a principled stand against it and followed the courage of her convictions.

Taking a stand is never easy, especially a public stand. Abraham and Sarah were revered in their generation and known far beyond the land of Canaan. They would have been popular with the locals and known for righteousness and a peaceful way of living. So when Hagar decided to flee from their tent, the news would have reached the ears of everyone from Canaan back to Egypt. It would have been noised abroad that all was not well in the Abraham household.

By running away, Hagar would undoubtedly have left Sarah and Abraham shell-shocked, even embarrassed, especially given that Hagar was expecting Abraham's baby. It proved a masterstroke! Yet it demanded courage also. The wilderness of Beersheba would have been no place for a pregnant woman and her baby to try to cope alone.

Try to imagine the conversation between Abraham and Sarah

following Hagar's daring departure.

Abraham: 'What on earth happened here today, Sarah?'

Sarah: 'You told me I could do what I liked with Hagar.'

Abraham: 'You didn't have to push her over the edge, though; now look what's happened – she's run off with our child.'

Sarah: 'I know, Abraham, I'm sorry, truly I am.'

Many Christian writers point to Hagar's weakness in this situation, highlighting how she ran away from trouble, and it's easy to see why this is so. Regardless, I do not believe Hagar was running away due to any lack of courage or fortitude. On the contrary, in her own, quiet, dignified way, Hagar had quite possibly decided to take a stand against what she saw as injustice and cruel treatment from a lady who publicly would have had a reputation for being kind, godly, and supposedly her friend. While everyone on the outside would have regarded Sarah as the 'perfect Christian', so to speak – although of course this was way before the time of Christ – privately she was not behaving like one. Hagar was probably treated better by pagans in Egypt than by Sarah in Canaan.

Enough was enough! The bullying had to stop! A stand had to be taken!

We live in a world today where it appears every person seems to want to stand up for their rights. Christians have become increasingly concerned that they are being marginalised for holding to their belief that the Bible has been given without error and is the fully inspired and infallible Word of God. It is also the supreme and final authority in all matters of faith and conduct, and contending for the faith can produce some serious consequences.

There's understandable pressure today on Christians and Christian leaders to take a stand about many issues – things such as abortion, human trafficking, homosexuality, lack of freedom of speech, and the rise of false religions. We live in a culture where those who shout loudest seem to get heard the most. This trend has therefore led to a tendency where many Christians feel the need to be vocal.

While it's never wrong to take a stand against injustice, if we hope to impact our generation for God, 'how' and 'why' we take that stand needs to be considered first. For example, what does it mean to take a stand for Jesus?

Naturally we assume that speaking out against immorality is taking a stand for Christ. But when Jesus Himself was asked to respond to the hard questions of His own day, rather than speak out he would often remain silent and wasn't forced to go there. He often avoided political matters in order to preach the gospel. That didn't mean He was soft on sin, but He wouldn't be drawn into confrontations. He addressed the issue in a better way.

When a woman had been caught in the act of adultery, Jesus just sat down and wrote on the ground. He took time out before addressing the situation in a calm manner and asking if the woman's accusers were themselves without sin. One by one they all left and the problem was solved.

Why?

Jesus knew darkness can never overcome the light. Christians are actually not called to *stand up*, they are called to *stand out*!

We are to live with our true identity as God's people, allowing our lives to be transformed by Him and displaying the truth that living God's way works for us as individuals, for our families, and can bring positive change to our communities. We do not need to continually shout about how we are a Christian and how much we believe in our faith. Our lives should automatically make that statement for us.

Jesus said so in the Sermon on the Mount: 'Ye are the salt of the earth: but if the salt have lost his savour, wherewith shall it be salted? It is thenceforth good for nothing, but to be cast out, and to be trodden under foot of men. Ye are the light of the world. A city that is set on a hill cannot be hid. Neither do men light a candle, and put it under a bushel, but on a candlestick; and it giveth light unto all that are in the house. Let your light so shine before men, that they may see your good works, and glorify your Father which is in heaven' (Matthew 5:13–16).

Notice Jesus speaks of Christians as being 'salt' and 'light' which produces the fruit of 'good works', or 'kind actions'.

I'm reminded of the story of when Jesus spoke to the Roman authority Pilate, and when Paul addressed Festus and King Agrippa; they did so with respect, humility and kindness. They were all too aware that the people they were conversing with were lost and in need of a saviour, so they spoke kindly to them and treated them honestly. So impressed was King Agrippa with Paul's witness he declared, 'You almost persuade me to become a Christian' (Acts 26:28, NKJV).

The 'Portrait of a Christian' by Beatrice Clelland is one of my favourite illustrations regarding actions being more powerful than words: It goes:

Not only in the words you say,
Not only in your deeds confessed.
But in the most unconscious way is Christ expressed.
Is a beatific smile?
A holy light upon your brow?
Oh no, I saw His presence when you laughed just now.
To me was not the truth you taught,
To you so clear, to me so dim.

But when you came to me
You brought a sense of Him.
And from His light He beckons me
And from your lips His love is shed
Till I lose sight of you
And see the Christ instead.[2]

Many a Christian witness, however, has proved unsuccessful due to an aggressive stand being taken. While the motive may have been right, the method was inappropriate.

A poignant example of this misplaced zeal is found in the story of James and John in the book of Luke. One day, when the enemies of Christ, the Samaritans, did not receive Jesus, James and John asked if they could 'command fire to come down from heaven and consume them, just as Elijah did?' (Luke 9:54, NKJV) to which Jesus rebuked them, then replied, 'You do not know what manner of spirit you are of. For the Son of Man did not come to destroy men's lives but to save them' (Luke 9:55,56, NKJV).

Again Christ points out that peace, not anger, is God's way. He speaks about a 'manner of spirit' we are to possess. Anger and aggression, as we covered in the previous chapter, no matter what the excuse, is not the fruit of the Spirit or righteousness.

No doubt Jesus was impressed with the zeal and loyalty shown by James and John towards the Master; nevertheless, He definitely appears to question the methods they employed in taking a stand against the enemies of Christ. The words of John 3:16 are often quoted without adding the following verse, which is itself a powerful declaration for God. It reads: 'For God did not send His Son into the world to condemn the world, but that the world through Him might be saved' (John 3:17, NKJV).

A witness that is directly confrontational or violent in either actions or words becomes counterproductive to the ultimate goal of a Christian, which is to lead people to the love of God. Witnessing is often so much more effective when it is carried out peacefully and with a calm and gentle spirit. This may appear as weakness, but it is, in fact, strength. It may appear foolishness, but it is great wisdom.

This doesn't mean we are to be silent, especially in a generation where the need to speak up and speak often is required, but in a world full of traps and tests, we must consider more carefully the 'why' and indeed the 'how' when it comes to taking a stand for God.

Martin Luther King said: 'There comes a time when silence is a betrayal'. There is a time to speak and a time to keep silent and when the time to speak comes we must trust God to add authority and conviction to our words. Justice often takes time, but when a stand is taken, especially a peaceful one, God is with us and evil is stopped in its tracks, if only for a season. The apostle Paul wrote: 'and having done all, to stand. Stand therefore …' (Ephesians 6:13,14).

Notice Hagar – who, remember, was not considered a 'child of God' – didn't become violent when provoked by Sarah. She didn't retaliate. She didn't respond with similar abuse or taunts to Sarah's provocation. She just withdrew for a while to let things calm down. There were no fisticuffs, no shouting or brawling, just a withdrawal by Hagar to let the dust settle.

Mahatma Gandhi once commented:

'Non-violence is the greatest force at the disposal of mankind. It is mightier than the mightiest weapon of destruction devised by the ingenuity of man.'[3]

This approach is what Jesus preached during the Sermon on the Mount: 'Ye have heard that it hath been said, An eye for an eye, and a tooth for a tooth: But I say unto you, That ye resist not evil: but whosoever shall smite thee on thy right cheek, turn to him the other also. And if any man will sue thee at the law, and take away thy coat, let him have thy cloak also' (Matthew 5:38–40).

There's nothing like a dose of time and space to make one think. Couples who have gone through marital difficulties understand this principle. They have separated for a time when one person couldn't take any more and left the marital home, but after a period of reflection by both parties common sense prevails and the marriage can be restored. Why? Both had time to consider their ways.

When we find ourselves in a hostile environment and being oppressed, when there's injustice and prejudice and persecution evident, taking a stand and even withdrawing from certain situations gives our aggressor time to reflect, and gives God time to redirect.

I wonder what Hagar's reasoning was when she fled the home of Abraham and Sarah. Was Hagar hoping at a later stage for a similar outcome of peace and unity and restored relations between her and Sarah, or was she seriously considering never going back? Maybe it was an impulsive move by Hagar to flee from Sarah; now that she was experiencing the reality of life in the wilderness, did she begin to question her initial decision to run away in the first place? Or was this a tactical move, hoping the 'penny would drop', with Sarah remembering the harsh treatment she had inflicted on Hagar?

Whatever, there was a personal cost as Hagar took her stand against discrimination and inequality. It required determination and personal sacrifice to confront wrongdoing, but she had simply had enough! Hagar wasn't prepared to tolerate any more of Sarah's in-house harassment, so the Bible says: 'And when Sarai dealt hardly with her, she fled from her face' (Genesis 16:6). By running away she was drawing a line in the sand, and drawing attention to something which there was more than a hint of in Sarah's unsympathetic behaviour towards Hagar – something which is still too widespread in our own generation today – the scourge of racial bigotry.

For further thought, prayer and reflection

• How did Hagar take her stand against Sarah?
• Why do you think Hagar was forced to run away from Canaan?
• Why did Sarah mistreat Hagar?

Reflecting on how Hagar reacted to Sarah's mistreatment of her:

• Have you ever had to take a stand?
• Do you need to take a stand against bullying or intimidation?
• If so, how do you propose to do this?
• In what way should we take a stand for Jesus?

Notes

1. Martin Luther, *Strength to Love* (New York: Harper & Row, 1963).
2. https://joniewp.wordpress.com/poetry/portrait-of-a-Christian/.
3. brainyquote.com.

Nine:
The Rise Again of Racism

The only tired I was, was tired of giving in.
(Rosa Parks)[1]

One of the most renowned church pulpits in Northern Ireland is not found inside a building. Instead, the Wayside Pulpit is situated directly outside Stormont Presbyterian Church – a landmark that has stood since 1931 on the Upper Newtownards Road in Belfast.

The church sits adjacent to the Stormont parliament buildings, the spot where major political decisions are taken on a daily basis. The signpost has become a constant talking point and has been viewed by thousands of people who travel past the church every day.

Over the years there have been many memorable and interesting messages at this junction; the most notable, perhaps, in May 2014, when the weekly catchphrase read – 'God Loves All Races'. It was designed for the Giro d'Italia – an international cycling event in Northern Ireland – yet it did much more than simply connect with a cycle race. It also helped calm tensions at a time when racist incidents were noticeably on the increase. In fact, if ever a nation received a timely message, this was it. Four words – God Loves All Races – spoke eloquently and profoundly to a society that finds it easier to condemn than to show consideration for others who do not share the same values and beliefs.

Sadly, in Northern Ireland racism has become the new sectarianism. War is still being waged, but no longer solely against either Catholics or Protestants. Today's targets are black people, religious groups, and foreigners and immigrants from various continents around the globe. Regrettably, in Northern Ireland, there are at least two racist incidents and more than one race hate crime reported every day.

These incidents reveal much about the kind of civilisation we now live in, especially regarding the extent of the racist problem not just in Northern Ireland, of course, but much further afield. The motivation for the attacks appears to be racial hatred and ethnic cleansing, something which dates back centuries, of course, even to Bible days.

For example, was Sarah guilty of making cruel racist taunts about Hagar's Egyptian upbringing? I don't believe this view is stretching a point too far; on the contrary, it's more than conceivable that the mistreatment of her maidservant included some form of racism.

Sarah – a sincere worshipper of Jehovah God – was deeply unhappy that an Egyptian woman who worshipped foreign gods, and someone who was regarded as being outside of the covenant of God, was suddenly carrying what they all might have regarded as the 'child of promise'. How dare she assume such a position!

Afraid she would gain power, influence and standing within the Canaanite society, Sarah's worst emotions surfaced and she chose to drive her maidservant out of the house.

Yet isn't exactly the same thing happening today? Foreign immigrants are being hounded out of their properties and told to go back to where they came from due to fear that they will 'take jobs', 'gain power', and eventually 'take over'.

Despite the era of a 'shared future' and the dawn of a 'new' Northern Ireland, attacks on the properties of foreign nationals have intensified for these very reasons. The attackers paint racist graffiti onto the property, ahead of smashing doors and windows, before fleeing.

A Lithuanian woman whose business was burned down in Belfast in 2015 is one such example. She arrived in Ireland as a teenager, built up a thriving business, employing young people and boosting the local economy, yet is viewed by some as an 'immigrant beggar. Foreign immigrants require acceptance, understanding and support, not further disapproval. Like this Lithuanian woman, the majority of foreign immigrants are mostly law-abiding and hard-working people.

Kofi Annan, who served as the seventh secretary general of the United Nations from January 1997 to December 2006, said:

'Ignorance and prejudice are the handmaidens of propaganda. Our mission, therefore, is to confront ignorance with knowledge, bigotry with tolerance, and isolation with the outstretched hand of generosity. Racism can, will, and must be defeated.'[2]

Yet, sadly, there are still elements in Northern Ireland and in the UK and also further afield, who have great difficulty in accommodating any sort of difference in society.

For example, bananas are still being thrown at black soccer players throughout the world and racist chants are heard at major sports venues throughout Europe. In the USA, despite the election of the first-ever black President, racist tweets are constantly being exposed in political, sporting and religious circles.

While racism is on the rise again and has economic, political and social implications, the difference between current practice and biblical truth shows it to be primarily a moral and spiritual issue. The Bible doesn't deal with the race problem as we know it in our time, but it gives some very important principles which can be applied to race relations.

In the Old Testament, for example, we are informed that humanity was created in the image of God and therefore every human is of infinite worth. (Genesis 1:27). In the book of Acts, all human beings are a single family and have a common origin (Acts 17:24,26), while Jesus Christ died for the redemption of every person regardless of race or nationality (John 3:16).

Though racial and religious prejudice is rising, the Bible outlines how God's intention is for all cultures to live together in harmony through the gospel of Jesus Christ. God is no respecter of persons. James wrote, 'My brethren, have not the faith of our Lord Jesus Christ, the Lord of glory, with respect of persons' (James 2:1).

The word 'respect' here is translated as 'partiality'. God is grieved when we disrespect or mistreat someone because of their nationality, disability, weaknesses, poverty or the colour of their skin. Dave Willis wrote: 'God created our skin tones with beautiful variety, but all of our souls are the same colour.'[3]

While some may choose to discriminate against their fellow human beings and wish to keep them on the outside looking in,

God never does. The Bible clearly states believers of all ethnic backgrounds are in the family of God, brothers and sisters together.

Malachi wrote: 'Don't all of us have one Father? Didn't one God create us?' (Malachi 2:10, HCSB).

Regarding who will be in the kingdom, Luke says: 'they will come from east and west and from north and south, and will recline at the table in the kingdom of God' (Luke 13:39, NASB). Paul speaks of 'one body … one Lord, one faith, one baptism; one God and Father of all' (Ephesians 4:4–6, NKJV).

The power of the gospel does not turn people against others; it enables Christians to overcome racial prejudice in the same way Peter taught: 'God has shown me that I should not call any person … unclean' (Acts 10:28, ESV).

The following incident took place during the mid-1950s, yet sadly due to the rise of racial hatred in the twenty-first century, it sounds like a current event. Inspired by the leadership of Martin Luther King, in the month of December 1955, an ordinary black woman named Rosa Parks tackled racial intolerance when, on a bus, she refused to give up her seat to a white man.

On the bus that day, Mrs Parks audaciously initiated a new era in the American quest for freedom and equality. Some of her quotes remain legendary, especially the one where she famously remarked:

> People always say that I didn't give up my seat because I was tired but that isn't true. I was not tired physically or no more tired than I usually was at the end of a working day. I was not old, although some people have an image of me being old then. I was 42. No, the only tired I was, was tired of giving in.[4]

Mrs Parks, who died in 2005 at the age of ninety-two, was,

throughout her life, a formidable individual, one who'd reached the stage where she plainly refused to tolerate racial discrimination due to the colour of her skin. A youth leader of the local branch of the National Association for the Advancement of Coloured People (NAACP), along with her husband, Raymond, a barber, the couple had worked for many years to improve the lot of black Americans in the southern United States where rigid segregation laws had been in force since the end of the Civil War in 1865.

The brave actions of Rosa Parks one day on a bus in Montgomery, Alabama, forced many white people to acknowledge their own prejudices and reminded everyone that love is stronger than hate. She was just an ordinary woman coming home from an ordinary job, but her courage in refusing to give up her seat led to extraordinary things.

In order to stand up, she sat down and the world listened.

What an incentive for anyone who feels too unimportant or too uneducated to make a difference in stamping out racism even within our own society. In her words:

> When I got on the bus that day I had no idea that history was being made. I was only thinking about getting home. But I had to make up my mind. After many years of being a victim … not giving up my seat, and whatever I had to face afterwards, wasn't important … I felt the Lord would give me the strength to endure whatever I had to face. It was time for someone to stand up, or in my case, sit down.[5]

We all possess the potential to make a difference in life, but such potential must also be accompanied by courage and persistence and great belief in our own convictions. Courage isn't just about being brave. Courage is daring to do what's right despite the weakness of our flesh and the consequences which might follow. Courage is making a sacrifice for the benefit of others. And it will take immense courage to confront the growing epidemic of racism within the twenty-first century. It may cost us our popularity, position, even our financial security, but if that is the price in emphasising how God loves His creation then so be it. When it comes to racism in society, we must stand shoulder to shoulder with our oppressed fellow human beings of a different culture or skin colour.

Racism isn't just a continual problem in countries such as America where racist incidents occur almost daily; it's a global problem having now subverted many other countries.

In the UK, for example, in 2015, *The Independent* newspaper in London made known the findings of a new report which highlighted the difficulties experienced by people living on the periphery of society. It reported that hate crimes motivated by racism, religion and homophobia have notably increased in London in just over a year. Faith-related offences alone are also on the increase according to the *Evening Standard*, and incidents against disabled people have shot up dramatically. *The Telegraph* reported that the number of suspected race hate crimes taking place on UK railways is also rising. These figures were revealed following a freedom of information request after Chelsea football fans were videoed singing racist chants on a train and forcing three young Asian women and a black man to leave the carriage on the London Euston to Manchester Piccadilly train.

So many people in the world today are made to feel second-rate due to the colour of their skin or as a result of their ethnic and religious background. Since the start of the millennium, growing hostility to immigrants and widespread Islamophobia has set community relations back by decades, both in America and in Europe. One in three Britons now admit to being racially prejudiced. Racism has become a growing global problem again. A friend of mine stated: 'There's a bigot in all of us', yet there shouldn't be.

The senselessness of racial hatred was most tragically illustrated with the sickening shooting of many people at the Charleston Emanuel African Methodist Episcopal Church in 2015 by Dylann Roof. The massacre in Charleston by Roof was not, however, an isolated hate crime carried out by a mentally ill racist in South Carolina. It is concurrently representative and starkly indicative of the rampant racism structurally embedded in both America and across the world.

Is it not time to face up to present-day prejudices which lead to so much conflict in our society? Surely the time has come to put away the spirit of 'invincibility' which inhibits society from empathising with others and understanding those same historical and modern-day bigotries?

Racism isn't just an issue for Americans; it's an issue for the rest of the world also. If such extreme prejudices are not dealt with, it will invariably lead to further racial and religious hatred and violence in the coming decades.

In 2015, *The Guardian* newspaper highlighted the fact that the Charleston incident was not unusual; rather an evidence of the violence being waged against black communities and religious groups. This form of hatred and bigotry has been prevalent in America since the first Africans were kidnapped and forcibly transported there in the fifteenth century as slaves under deplorable, inhumane conditions. Over 500 years later, racial hatred and the subject of slavery – which we covered earlier – is indeed ominously raising its ugly head again.

Sarah may not have been guilty of some of the above-mentioned crimes, but anywhere there is even a hint of racism, strife, trouble and great suffering is just around the corner.

Racial bigotry and hate crimes are committed every day and the sad fact is, most people may not even be aware they are committing these offences. Racial hatred has been bred into them from birth or they've just learned to hate their fellow human beings somewhere along the way. Whether this is due to bad theology, ignorant preaching, prejudice or being misguided isn't quite clear, but the impact can be profound on those who are targeted. *Racial bigotry is wrong. It always has been wrong and it always will be wrong!*

It must be opposed again in the same way Martin Luther King refused to accept racism and religious bigotry of any description in his own generation. He courageously stood for the freedom of all peoples. He took a stand against racism, religious intolerance, injustice, slavery, discrimination, exploitation of the weak and the poor, and the result was that other great liberators and champions of freedom followed.

Nelson Mandela said: 'No one is born hating another person because of the colour of his skin, or his background, or his religion. People must learn to hate, and if they can learn to hate, they can be taught to love, for love comes more naturally to the human heart than its opposite.'[6]

Hagar's account reminds us how the gospel of Jesus Christ transcends all religious barriers and is for everyone who will receive it. God's command to every believer is to reach out to people of all faiths and all backgrounds with the good news of the gospel. This is evident by one of Christ's last commands to His followers: 'Go ye therefore, and teach all nations, baptizing them in the name of the Father, and of the Son, and of the Holy Ghost' (Matthew 28:19).

The story of Hagar therefore teaches us a lesson, which I believe needs to be revealed again to this generation, namely – God is not an elitist. His love is much bigger, wider and higher than the confines of one skin colour, one church, one faith, and one theological viewpoint.

Have you been a victim of race hate? Has it driven you out of a job, a church, even a country? Do you feel discriminated against? Are you lost, wandering in a wilderness and searching for purpose? Then know that no matter where you are, God can find you and restore you. God is nearer to you than you might realise. God is not a racist!

For further thought, prayer and reflection

- Was Sarah guilty of cultural pride or racism, or both?
- Do you feel you are kind to strangers in general, or do you not really care about them?
- If you search your heart, do you find any trace of racism? What do you think God feels about racism? Be honest with yourself, and Him.
- What can you do to help prevent racism within your own community? How can you make a foreign national feel more welcome in your country?
- Are you or have you been the victim of race hate crimes? How did you or are you dealing with this?
- What does God's Word have to say regarding race relations?

Notes

1. en.m.wickiquote.org.
2. goodreads.com.
3. DaveWillis.org.
4. en.m.wickiquote.org.
5. books.google.co.uk.
6. goodreads.com.

Ten:
I Will Find You

'If I ascend into heaven, You are there; If I make my bed in hell, behold, You are there.'
(Psalm 139:8, NKJV)

Whether you're a teenager trying to escape the discipline of Mum and Dad – and we've all been there – or a pregnant mother like Hagar fleeing from family intimidation, or a refugee running from a violent and wartorn country, being on the run is no laughing matter.

How will you find employment? Where will you sleep? What will you get to eat? If you are pregnant or have children, heaven help you! How will you provide for them?

Yet isn't this the current experience of millions of people in our world every day just as it was for Hagar, Sarah's maidservant, as she scampered into the wilderness away from Sarah's browbeating? Millions of people are forced today to run away from horrendous and perilous circumstances!

In addition to meaning stranger, the Hebrew name Hagar also means 'one who flees' or 'one who seeks refuge'. This was Hagar during her separate wilderness experiences; a woman on the run and isolated from any real form of security, she must have cut an extremely lonely figure. Broke, disgruntled and disgusted, rejected, refused and redundant, she wandered aimlessly through the desert.

In many ways, Hagar's first spell in the wilderness – and especially the dilemma surrounding her impromptu return to the home of Abraham and Sarah – illustrates entirely the plight of many similar refugee women in the world today. With child, or responsible for other children, and unable to fend for themselves, these people are trapped and torn between their love for their birthplace and a foreign culture they've been forced into.

As stated, Hagar's name means 'stranger' and there are many strangers in our world today; people estranged from their countries, families, and religious brethren. The question is: as the migrant crisis in Europe deepens, and thousands of strangers pour into various countries, how will they be received? Are they going to be viewed as a burden, or can we turn the situation into a blessing? Are they likely to be viewed with suspicion or will they be warmly welcomed and given the best of hospitality? The Bible points out how Christians, in particular, are not to reject the stranger because in so doing they may be rejecting the messenger of God. 'Be not forgetful to entertain strangers: for thereby some have entertained angels unawares' (Hebrews 13:2). Due to the global crisis involving refugees, only in recent times have people understood the difference between the term 'migrant' and the term 'refugee'. The Oxford Dictionary defines a migrant as 'a person who moves from one place to another in order to find work'. It explains a refugee like this: 'a person who has been forced to leave their country in order to escape'. Other translations refer to refugees as being 'displaced' and 'in great danger'.[1] Refugees therefore require help and assistance.

Many refugees and people of various backgrounds and situations have been 'left to die' today; and so grave is their situations they don't even possess legal status, making it almost impossible to access basic services, and exposing them to exploitation. It's reported that even when there is legal status, urban refugees face frequent harassment by police, including beatings, intimidation, illegal detention, and demands for bribes. Refugee women are particularly vulnerable to sexual violence, human smuggling and trafficking.

Having risked everything for a new life elsewhere, these poor souls are caught between not being able to provide for themselves, the fear of aggression, and the thought of having to return under the control of an oppressive regime in the nation they had to originally flee from. They are stuck between a rock and a hard place!

Take, for example, the situation in Calais, France, where the scenes have often been disturbing in recent years. An unofficial camp nearby houses hundreds of desperate refugees, including children, who have fled war or poverty, or who have simply decided the UK offers more opportunity than the homes they've left behind – usually in the Middle East, Africa and Central Asia. This camp is known as the 'Jungle' and contains few of the amenities of a real refugee camp, such as plentiful water and sturdy shelters.

On 18 June 2015, UNHCR (The UN Refugee Agency) revealed that worldwide displacement was at the highest level ever recorded. It said that the number of people forcibly displaced at the end of 2014 had risen to a staggering 59.2 million compared with 51.2 million a year earlier and 37.5 million a decade ago. Tragically, half of the refugees in the world are children. Many of them are abandoned and seeking shelter, yet often these vulnerable infants fall into the hands of criminal groups.

Misconceptions about refugees are common. For example, many of these people are often thought to be dwelling in tents in a desert, but this doesn't give an accurate picture of what life is like for millions of refugees in the twenty-first century.

While this may well have been Hagar's experience as she sought refuge in the wilderness of Beersheba, it isn't the experience of many refugees today. According to the United Nations Refugee Agency, almost half of the world's 10.5 million refugees reside in urban areas, in cities like Bangkok in Thailand, Amman in Jordan, and Nairobi in Kenya.

While many go to cities to find some form of normal community life, the fact is they encounter the complete opposite, having to undergo provocation, violence and, of course, poverty. Refugees fleeing conflict or natural disaster are unable to return home, and so they must build lives in their newly adopted cities. This is quite a quandary, especially for families. In fact, it can be an existence which produces suffering and fear of unimaginable proportions.

An astonishing one million Syrians have been forced to leave their lives behind to escape the war, crossing the borders to neighbouring Jordan, Lebanon, Turkey and Iraq. As many fear they might be stopped if they appear to be on the run, the refugees carry little more than they can fit in their pockets or the folds of their clothes. They have brought with them what is closest to their hearts, seeking sanctuary from the Syrian conflict in refugee camps and temporary shelter. The appalling sight of hundreds of thousands of refugees fighting to board trains in Europe in order to get to Germany in September 2015 brought home just how many people have been forced to flee their normal environments. Thousands of desperate migrants and refuges marched 150 miles along motorways in Hungary to get to Austria after the Hungarian PM told them they were not welcome. After four days of being forcibly camped outside a train station in central Budapest, hundreds gathered what few belongings they had to march across Europe. Some walked for six hours nonstop in 80C heat. The pictures being beamed around the world of children clutching dolls and teddy bears while clinging on to their parents' hands was a harrowing sight indeed. All these people wanted was freedom and somewhere safe to live and work.

Thankfully, aid agencies and charities do a magnificent job in supporting these people but so, too, does the church in general. God's people are spread out all over the world in mission fields reaching out to these poor souls, assisting them where they are and also attempting to help them to return to their former lands and a culture they are more familiar with. Even in their pain, loneliness, fear and sorrow, the love of God is tracking them and blessing them. God cares about the state of refugees – and so should we.

In the same way, God also cares for millions of spiritual refugees today, people the Bible interestingly refers to as 'backsliders' – men and women who could be termed 'On the Runs'. Many Christians don't like the term 'backslider' but it is a biblical word! The phrase originated from the book of Hosea, when the people consulted images and not the divine Word. Hosea writes: 'Israel slideth back as a backsliding heifer' – It's interesting that he added the words, 'the LORD will feed them ... in a large place' (Hosea 4:16).

Isn't the mercy of God something special? Even in our disobedience God feeds us, forgives us and enlarges us! In other words, God loves the backslider – the spiritual refugee, on the run and out of fellowship.

Why?

He feels their pain and understands their hurts. These individuals once attended a church they called home, but due to suffering injustice and rejection, many wounded souls have chosen to flee into the wilderness seeking refuge. The problem is, there is no shelter in the wilderness. It brings little comfort and no security. What we sometimes think will end up becoming a place of sanctuary, instead becomes an even worse environment than where we came from. Like the parable told by Jesus in the book of Luke about the prodigal son who found himself on the run from his father's house and ended up in the far country, many spiritual refugees find themselves without so much as a scrap of bread to eat and bottle of water to drink. Having 'left church', these former worshippers end up starved of the Word of God and find themselves a long way from their Father's house.

Yet God still has a great purpose for the spiritual refugee. He loves them and wants them to listen to his voice calling them home again, just as Hagar listened during her own period of absconding.

The Bible records that as she wandered in the wilderness, an angel came before her and spoke to her, telling her what she should do. 'The angel of the LORD found Hagar near a spring in the desert; it was the spring that is beside the road to Shur. And he said, "Hagar, servant of Sarai, where have you come from, and where are you going?" "I'm running away from my mistress Sarai," she answered. Then the angel of the LORD told her, "Go back to your mistress and submit to her"' (Genesis 16:7–9, NIV 1984).

This caused conflict within Hagar's spirit. The angel told her to return. Hagar wanted to flee.

Of course, it's a normal reaction to want to escape from any form of persistent rejection and oppression, regardless of where it takes place. Sometimes we can't take any more, and this was Hagar. But, spiritually speaking, God's way is always restoration, not isolation.

Hagar was on the road to Shur which was the road to Egypt, so, clearly Hagar appears to be finished with all things related to Abraham's God. She seemed to be heading back to more familiar territory; to her own culture, religion and people. Following her experiences with Abraham and Sarah, I imagine she'd had a 'belly-full' of prophecies and pined for a quiet life with people she used to be acquainted with. Hagar had lost her way, but God's eyes were upon her and her situation. She was not only running from God's purpose; she was running back to a place where people worshipped idols and foreign gods, yet God cared about this and was determined to reassign her. She was running away from God's people, from God's house and most of all, perhaps, she was running away from God Himself!

After Romania was liberated from Nicolae Ceausescu's brutal communist regime in 1989, some years later the people complained that their long, sought-after freedom had come at a hefty price. As the rich got richer and the poor became poorer, this left many peasants wishing they were back living in the days of communism. The poor were overlooked and became forgotten. One lady stated: 'At least in the communist period we were assured of a loaf of bread per day and some rice – now we have nothing.' The promised prosperity attached to the so-called 'new Romania' hadn't been the experience of this lady or many other Romanians, so naturally they began to look towards the road to Shur and recall how things used to be.

Many believers and religious people tend to do the same thing. When life in the church or their preferred place of worship fails to live up to expectations of freedom and liberty, when persecution and mistreatment occurs, there's a tendency to remember the former life and imagine it to be more glamorous than it actually was. The very thing they had been delivered from becomes attractive again and so they set off in the wrong direction.

Perhaps you are on the run from some Christian denomination, or have suffered demonization of your character due to persecution by the people of God. Maybe, like Hagar, you've had enough of God's people and think returning to Egypt, so to speak, will simplify your life and make everything OK. So you have fled into the wilderness to find yourself and seek refuge. While you are going one way, have you ever considered God may wish to take you in another direction – back again to where you came from?

What am I saying?

If your purpose was in Israel, why are you heading to Egypt? Turn around and start heading back!

Consider the amazing story of Jonah in the Old Testament. Here was a man who knew in his heart that he was to go to the city of Nineveh to preach God's message, yet instead he decided to try to run away from the purpose of God for his life. Jonah, in fact, went to extraordinary lengths to avoid the call of God, which included booking a cruise to another destination. But the Bible records that while he was aboard the ship, a mighty storm came and, suddenly, Jonah was washed overboard and landed inside the belly of a great fish, which held him captive for three days and three nights before finally releasing him unto the shore. Jonah was then told to return to the very place he ran away from –

Nineveh – and to preach against it.

We can run, but we can't hide! God will always find us, no matter where we are.

Jonah was not the first person to discover that no matter how hard we try, we can't run away from God. God will find us only because He loves us and desires the best for us. He is a loving and compassionate God, One who has a purpose for our lives. David knew the reality of this truth, stating: 'If I ascend up into heaven, thou art there; if I make my bed in hell, behold, thou art there' (Psalm 139:8).

We can run from any situation we choose, we can take a stand like Hagar, but when God's purpose is for us to be in Israel, not Egypt, He will be waiting for us at our new address. God loves and cares for the spiritual refugee and longs to see them return to their Father's house. Such was the love of the father for the prodigal son that he rushed out to greet him and threw his loving arms around him. He was just so glad that the son had chosen to return.

Similarly, God is just waiting for the spiritual refugee, the backslider to return to church and to the Christian faith, especially if you have been separated from your brethren. I think I understand why God wants us to persevere with relationships within the church and humbly submit and return, even in relation to what we see as challenging brethren. It's because God is Himself a restoring God, a God of peace and unity and fellowship; a God of forgiveness and a God of numerous chances.

God smiles when we face the people we have difficulty with and confront the issues at hand and find solutions. He is calling us to work harder at our relationships; not to quit and run away unless absolutely necessary. Rather than run from our responsibilities, God wants us to face up to them in faith and obedience. He also longs to see the wounded and backslidden sheep return to its fold.

In the same way, the task of the angel assigned to Hagar was to 'turn her right around' and send her back to the place of her abuser – Sarah's home – a daunting and difficult prospect, of course, for the utterly dependent and now vulnerable Hagar. Yet that was God's will for her life.

For further thought, prayer and reflection

- Are you aware of the pain and suffering being experienced by many refugees around the world today? Are you in a position to help any of these people? Where do many of them mainly reside?
- How does being a refugee affect young vulnerable women?
- Do you know any refugees or spiritual refugees (backsliders) who need to be encouraged and helped?

Note

1. oxforddictionaries.com.

Eleven:
Returning to the Scene of the Crime

Would not love see returning penitence afar off, and fall on its neck and kiss it?
(George Eliot)[1]

Most criminals would hardly wish to return to the scene of a crime. In the same way, no one wants to return to a place of hostility unless absolutely necessary, but Hagar was about to experience just this after a surprising appearance by the angel of God.

There's no record of just how long Hagar wandered in the wilderness before the angel appeared before her. Was it days, weeks, months? We don't know! But her spell away from the home of Abraham and Sarah must have been a frightening and lonely time of exile.

With no help and no support base, one can only imagine how this pregnant, impoverished Egyptian woman coped at that time. If she'd been crying to God for help in order to find direction for her life, then God certainly answered those cries with the words: 'I want you to return.'

The Bible records that the angel found Hagar by a spring of water in the wilderness along the road to Shur (Egypt) and told her to return to her mistress, Sarah.

This miraculous moment caused the pregnant and defenceless Hagar to declare, 'You are the God who sees.' The NIV renders this statement even more personal and enlightening in relation to Hagar's relationship with God – 'You are the God who sees me' (Genesis 16:13).

When we are singled out by God in such a loving, individual way, especially when the situation is quite desperate, it speaks much about the personal care God gives to all of His creation. The angel of the Lord had found Hagar in a wilderness by a fountain of water and opened her eyes; then met her need. She had discovered a well of water nearby known as Beer Lahai Roi, or the 'well of the living One who sees me'. God had proved how much He cared by calling out her name and position in life, affirming, 'Hagar, Sarah's maid' (Genesis 16:8).

God's angel even asked her where she was going, provoking the response from Hagar: 'I flee from the face of my mistress Sarai' (Genesis 16:8). To which the angel replied: 'Return to thy mistress, and submit thyself under her hands' (Genesis 16:9).

The instruction by the angel couldn't have been any clearer – go back to where you came from!

Hagar was commanded to reappear in a place of great hurt, turmoil and rejection, but significantly, she would not be going alone – God would be with her. Despite the immensity of this request by the angel, God was clearly with Hagar and would fill her with grace to complete her assignment. God unquestionably loved Hagar just as deeply and passionately as

He loved Abraham and Sarah.

While Isaac has always represented a picture of God's love for the church, Hagar has continually been portrayed as a magnificent portrait of God's love for the world, displayed in the plan He had for Hagar's life, too!

Nevertheless, the mere thought of going back to the scene of the crime – Sarah's home – must have filled Hagar's heart with huge apprehension. It was a momentous test in terms of Hagar's obedience regarding the purpose of God for her life. For example, her flesh wouldn't have wanted to return to a place where she suffered daily harassment. She was not only left wounded, but would have felt disappointed at the way things had been handled regarding the forthcoming birth of her child; hence, she'd lost all confidence in both Abraham and Sarah.

While Sarah may have been the main aggressor towards Hagar, Abraham, as the leader of the household, wouldn't have been blameless either, because clearly he'd failed to stop the abuse by saying nothing. Strangely, he turned a blind eye by ignoring discrimination and cruelty which was taking place right under his own roof. Abraham must have known Sarah's conduct towards Hagar was unfair, but he still did absolutely nothing about it.

The story depicts Sarah and Abraham as being very unsympathetic. Regarding her fleeing into the wilderness, it caused the thirteenth-century Spanish commentator Nahmanides to write:

Our mother (Sarah) transgressed by this affliction and Abraham did likewise by permitting her to do so. So God heard Hagar's affliction and gave her a son who would be 'a wild ass of a man' to afflict the seed of Abraham and Sarah with all kinds of affliction.[2]

In effect, the commentator Nahmanides is saying that Sarah's mistreatment of Hagar is a reason why Sarah's children would one day be persecuted by the descendants of Hagar, who we know today are the extreme followers of Islam. This incident, thousands of years ago, may well be the key to understanding many of our present-day troubles! Mistreating people always comes back to haunt us. Some Christians may find this hard to accept, believing they do not commit such wicked deeds and equally convinced that the root of world strife is always someone else's fault. This is spiritual pride which is covered in a later chapter.

Meanwhile, Abraham's uncharacteristic indifference to Hagar's pain, however, epitomises people today at all levels of authority, people in high-ranking positions who see injustices and discrimination and refuse to step in and exercise just leadership. Martin Luther King said,

'Injustice anywhere is a threat to justice everywhere.'[3]

Many influential individuals are fearful of personal criticism and media scrutiny; thus they allow dastardly deeds to go unpunished. They don't want to 'get their hands dirty' or 'jeopardise their own popularity', so they stay silent and permit others to endure shocking situations. Well over half a century after those words were spoken by Martin Luther King, injustice continues to abound throughout the world.

As the world is developing, many injustices are coming to light such as poverty, starvation, wrongful imprisonment, ignoring of the elderly, overlooking the needs of widows and orphans, racism, physical and verbal abuse, sex trafficking and war and grief, to name only a few. To turn the other way shows indifference to injustice.

While there is, of course, much love, joy and even redemption in this world, there is also ample suffering, heartache, and despair. Ask yourself, what constitutes injustice? Sometimes it can be standing up for what one believes to be right, only to then be persecuted and maligned for daring to take such a position. It can be turning a blind eye to those suffering beside you, or a lack of courage to help transform an unacceptable set of circumstances.

While Hagar wouldn't have been equal in terms of wifely status to Sarah, as his wife she would undoubtedly considered him a shepherd and therefore she would have looked to him for leadership and protection, but when he told Sarah to **deal** with her maidservant as she pleased, Hagar knew she was fighting a losing battle.

The Bible states: 'And Sarai said unto Abram, My wrong be upon thee: I have given my maid into thy bosom; and when she saw that she had conceived, I was despised in her eyes: the LORD judge between me and thee. But Abram said unto Sarai, Behold, thy maid is in thine hand; do to her as it pleaseth thee' (Genesis 16:5,6). Imagine being told by the angel of God that she must return to such an uncaring environment. Hagar would surely have preferred a brand-new start somewhere else. Besides, it would be embarrassing and humiliating, having to humble herself and revisit a place where she'd taken a decisive stand; then had to go back to it with her tail between her legs.

The only thing Hagar seemed to have accomplished in all of her self-inflicted isolation from the only family and community she had, was making a valid point. Sometimes making an important point is all many of us can hope to achieve in a ruthless world where change sometimes starts with the making of a point; then takes generations to get the point.

As Hagar contemplated her own humiliation, all sorts of thoughts must have come to mind.

I wonder, did she hear the imaginary voices of those back in Abraham's home environment saying:

'Didn't think she would stick the wilderness for long.'

'Yep, knew she'd come crawling back.'

'You can't fight City Hall.'

'She'll learn the hard way.'

Of course, this may not have been the case, but when you're cut off from your normal environment, thoughts like these do start to appear. Paranoia takes over and we begin to adopt an 'us against the world' mentality. The same people were probably praying for Hagar; Abraham and Sarah no doubt regretted her leaving in the first place, but the thought of returning after her lengthy retreat was still far from being an appetising thought.

Three words, spoken by the angel of the Lord to Hagar stand out in this part of the story – the words 'return', 'submit' and 'angel'.

We will examine in more detail the word 'angel' in the following chapter, but for now let's focus on the words 'return' and 'submit'. God's way is most often a way of restoration and humble submission. God regularly challenges us to persevere with people no matter how unkind they are; to work at difficult relationships and seek peace and unity wherever possible.

To return!

This was Hagar's challenge, given that her own purpose was not yet fulfilled in the home of Abraham and Sarah. God was sending her back to her post; to unfinished business – giving birth to Ishmael. Scared, nervous, and even hurt, Hagar was being sent back to the scene of the crime!

Matthew Henry's commentary states: 'Those who leave their space and duty must hasten their return, however mortifying so ever it be.'[4] In the same way that Hagar wandered in the wilderness, many of us wander away from God every day. Is God's angel speaking to you in your wilderness and pleading with you to return?

Is God trying to get your attention as you flee from His plans for your life? If you do return you will not find an angry and bitter God, which sadly is presented in too many places today. Instead you will encounter a loving, merciful Saviour – One who is just waiting to welcome you back into fellowship with Him and God's people.

In the words of the prophet Joel: 'And rend your heart, and not your garments, and turn unto the LORD your God: for he is gracious and merciful, slow to anger, and of great kindness, and repenteth him of the evil' (Joel 2:13).

We've all run away at times, but when God has a plan for our lives we don't get too far. Hagar was on the run, but God found her and asked her to return to a place of conflict – a house of strife and anger and jealousy. That hardly seems logical, or even fair, but this was what the angel of God – and the humility God – demanded of her. God doesn't always send us to attractive or obvious places. He was encouraging Hagar to submit to His will for her life.

The word 'submit' is defined as 'the action of accepting or yielding to a superior force or to the will or authority of another person.'[5] In other words, when the word 'submit' is used in the Bible, it refers not only to an attitude of obedience, cooperation and support. Without cooperation and support, things just don't work the way they should.

Are we similarly yielded and under the authority of Almighty

God? Do we 'submit' to His will or do we dig our heels in and refuse to obey?

The latter often happens when there is a clear lack of submission and presence of the Holy Spirit in our lives. Only the enablement of the Holy Spirit allows us to exhibit a beautiful spirit of submission, as Hagar ultimately displayed.

Despite being a foreigner in the eyes of Abraham and Sarah… despite being considered outside of the covenant of God… even with her Egyptian upbringing, Hagar was controlled by the Spirit of God and regardless of the difficulty of the task being presented to her, she obeyed the angel of the Lord. This is quite a challenge to Christians who often live in total disobedience to the Spirit of God. Sometimes God does insist we confront things which are hard physically, but in the best interests of our spirit. Hagar may not have been considered 'one of the saints', but she was submitted to God!

The angel of the Lord was not only about to invite Hagar, but Abraham and Sarah to put away their differences and reconcile for the sake of the child Ishmael and his purpose. The stage was being set for an unlikely but emotional reunion. The great English novelist, George Eliot, once said, 'Would not love see returning penitence afar off, and fall on its neck and kiss it?'[6]

There is something touching about repentance, forgiveness and a fresh start of this nature which comes from a submissive spirit. Someone has to be the first to back down from any confrontation in order for peace to be possible, and on this occasion it was Hagar. She was compelled to repent and return to her own 'scene of the crime' because God had a great purpose for her life. She hadn't yet completed her work in Canaan, and therefore had to return in order to fulfil God's divine plan – the birth of Ishmael!

This may be easily read in the Bible, but it wouldn't have been easily accomplished in reality by Hagar. This was a lady with nowhere left to hide and nowhere left to run. Penniless, poor and pregnant, she had no future and no home. For the second time she would have been a refugee entering Canaan and viewed as little more than a beggar!

For further thought, prayer and reflection

- What did the angel of the Lord tell Hagar to do when He appeared to her in the wilderness?
- Is God asking you to move on from or return to an unpleasant situation?
- Have you witnessed weak leadership which has allowed discrimination to flourish in your home, workplace or church? Consider ways as to how you can be effective in this situation.
- Name some of the injustices in our world today. Do you turn a blind eye to these things, or will you try to help prevent them from taking place?
- If God asked you to do something difficult, how submitted to him are you? Why not discuss this with others?
- What does God expect us to do when we encounter difficult people?

Notes

1. top100.net.
2. RabbiSacks.org.
3. brainyquote.com.
4. Matthew Henry's Concise Commentary, biblehub.com.
5. oxforddictionaries.com.
6. top100.net.

Twelve:
Do You Believe in Angels?

What a loving God we serve! Not only has He prepared a heavenly dwelling for us, but his angels also accompany us as we make transition from this world to the next. (David Jeremiah)[1]

We can't engage in the next part of Hagar's story – what happened after her return to Canaan – without, of course, acknowledging the supernatural event that helped get her there in the first place – a visitation from the angel of God.

On the run and wandering aimlessly in the wilderness, had the angel not appeared to this Egyptian woman, she would probably have faded into history and not been mentioned again. She certainly wouldn't have returned to Canaan. The likelihood is, she would have died in the wilderness, carrying her unborn child, and her story would never have touched our lives in the manner that it has. Mercifully, however, God sent an angel – His own personal messenger – to redirect Hagar's path and ensure that His purpose was fulfilled in her life.

I've chosen to explore the subject of angel visitation because so often we can read accounts like Hagar's in the Bible and completely fail to comprehend just how amazingly special these incidents were, and still are – certainly to those chosen for such an experience.

Statements like 'and the angel of the LORD found [Hagar] by a fountain of water in the wilderness' (Genesis 16:6) or, 'the angel of the Lord said unto her' (vv. 9,10,11) roll quickly off our tongues, almost as if angel visitations are considered a normal part of everyday life. Yet for most people, that's simply not the case. When was the last time you or I were visited by an angel?

Sadly there are some highly exaggerated accounts of people who claim to speak to angels on a daily basis, tales which totally spoil the beautiful and authentic visitations of angels which have taken place, not just in Bible days, but in modern times, too.

Incidents like these only discourage people who want to believe in the authenticity of angels and their purpose here on earth. Of course, no one speaks to angels every day and nor do angels suddenly jump out at us in a hotel lobby or a backstreet alley. Don't get me wrong, I believe in angels; I believe in them with all of my heart because I am convinced they've protected me on various occasions in my life; nevertheless, the reality is, many people will never be visited personally by an angel during their lifetime.

While the people throughout the centuries who have experienced a genuine visitation by an angel are not necessarily few in number, they are extremely privileged.

In Genesis 32 we read how the angels of God (plural) met Jacob. Later in verse 24 it says: 'And Jacob was left alone; and there wrestled a man with him until the breaking of the day' (Genesis 32:24). Note the words 'And Jacob was left alone'.

Angels don't normally appear to groups, but to individuals. What does this suggest to us? When we get alone with God, He has our individual attention and His presence is easier to recognise. This is where the supernatural can become normal. This is the place of God's visitation and the place where supernatural things we've been praying about take place!

When Moses returned from seeking God on the mountain, his face shining with the presence of God, he'd been alone with God for forty days. Similarly, when the angel came to Hagar, she was not at home with Abraham and Sarah amidst all of the hustle and bustle of everyday life in Canaan; she wasn't in a crowded, noisy, populated place, she was all alone in the wilderness – it was just her and God – but that's the place where she received her greatest-ever experience.

Jacob was all alone, too, when angels showed up to him. His story records that he wrestled with a man (an angel) – or was it a reincarnate Christ – until the breaking of day and would not give up until the Lord blessed him. Eventually Jacob received his blessing when God, through the angel of the Lord, changed his name from Jacob to Israel – meaning 'Prince with God' or 'triumphant with God'. He walked with a limp thereafter and there was a dramatic change in his life following this incident.

Jacob actually marked the very spot where he received his own privileged visitation by God's heavenly messengers. The Bible records: 'And Jacob called the name of the place Peniel: for I have seen God face to face, and my life is preserved' (Genesis 32:30).

This was also the experience of Gideon who himself received a visitation by an angel. Possessing no confidence or self-worth, Gideon was a beaten man until the angel appeared and told him he was a mighty man, specially selected and chosen by God. The Bible says: 'And the angel of the LORD appeared unto him, and said unto him, The LORD is with thee, thou mighty man of valour' (Judges 6:12). Gideon was never the same again.

Joshua was confronted by an angel near Jericho and told what to do regarding the enemies of God's people. At the birth of Jesus Christ, an angel of the Lord appeared to lowly shepherds – and the angel Gabriel brought the message to Mary that she was to have a baby. Abraham, Daniel and Peter all experienced visitations from angels, and God also used angels to rescue Abraham's nephew Lot.

Therefore Hagar was a most privileged woman, for not once, but twice, during her wilderness experiences, God sent an angel to Hagar. An Egyptian slave, Sarah's bitter rival, a 'heathen' – Hagar had one thing going for her that her mistress never seemed to experience in the same way – a personal revelation of God.

Angels are not exclusive to Bible stories like Hagar's, however. Throughout history, people have reported all sorts of encounters with angels. These reports have emerged from every corner of the globe and from every culture. Barbara's story is one such example.

Barbara was driving her six-year-old son, Benjamin, to his piano lesson. They were late, and Barbara was beginning to think she should have cancelled it. There was always so much to do, and Barbara, a night-duty nurse at the local hospital, had recently worked extra shifts. She was tired. The sleet storm and icy roads added to her tension. Maybe she should turn the car around. 'Mom,' Ben cried. 'Look!' Just ahead, a car had lost control on a patch of ice. As Barbara tapped the brakes, the other car spun wildly, rolled over, and then crashed sideways into a telephone pole. Barbara pulled over, skidded to a stop and threw open her door. Thank goodness she was a nurse –

she might be able to help these unfortunate passengers. Then she paused. What about Ben? She couldn't take him with her. Little boys shouldn't see scenes like the one she anticipated. But was it safe to leave him alone? What if their car were hit from behind? For a brief moment Barbara considered going on her way. Someone else was sure to come along. No! 'Ben, honey, promise me you'll stay in the car!' 'I will, Mommy,' he said as she ran, slipping and sliding towards the crash site. It was worse than she'd feared. Two girls of high school age were in the car. One, the blonde on the passenger side, was dead, killed on impact. The driver, however, was still breathing. She was unconscious and pinned in the wreckage. Barbara quickly applied pressure to the wound in the teenager's head while her practised eye catalogued the other injuries. A broken leg, maybe two, along with probable internal bleeding. But if help came soon, the girl would live. A trucker had pulled up and was calling for help on his cellular phone. Soon Barbara heard the ambulance sirens. A few moments later she surrendered her lonely post to rescue workers. 'Good job,' one said as he examined the driver's wounds. 'You probably saved her life, ma'am.' Perhaps, but as Barbara walked back to her car a feeling of sadness overwhelmed her, especially for the family of the girl who had died. Their lives would never be the same. Oh, God, why do such things have to happen? Slowly Barbara opened her car door. What should she tell Benjamin? He was staring at the crash site, his blue eyes huge. 'Mom,' he whispered, 'did you see it?' 'See what, honey?' she asked. 'The angel, Mom! He came down from the sky while you were running to the car. And he opened the door, and he took that girl out.' Barbara's eyes filled with tears. 'Which door, Ben?' 'The passenger side. He took the girl's hand, and they floated up to heaven together'. 'What about the driver?' Ben shrugged. 'I didn't see anyone else.' Later, Barbara was able to meet the families of the victims. They expressed their gratitude for the help she had provided. Barbara was able to give them something more – Ben's vision. There was no way he could have known what happened to either of the passengers. Nor could the passenger door have been opened; Barbara had seen its tangle of immovable steel herself. Yet Ben's account brought consolation to a grieving family. Their daughter was safe in heaven. And they would see her again.[2]

Angels are real and exist for many purposes, especially to lead people to God. Hebrews chapter one says of angels: 'Are they not all ministering spirits, sent forth to minister for them who shall be heirs of salvation?' (Hebrews 1:14).

The word angel literally means 'messenger' sent by God to aid the heirs of salvation. When Hagar was at her lowest ebb and desperately requiring help, the angel of the Lord miraculously appeared before her. The question has to be, why?

Why Hagar?

Why not Sarah?

Why send an angel to a heathen woman, a person Abraham's people wouldn't even have recognised as part of God's chosen congregation? Why did she not fade into oblivion and suffer alone? Isn't it because God loved Hagar with an everlasting love? Isn't it because He cared for this pregnant, abandoned Egyptian slave girl so much, He sent an angel to her side? Doesn't this prove the immensity of God's love for His creation? God loves you no matter where you live or which church you choose to attend. Even if you attend no church at all, the amazing news is that God still loves you and desires to see you turn to Him. The

Bible affirms this, declaring: 'The Lord is not slack concerning his promise, as some men count slackness; but is longsuffering to us-ward, not willing that any should perish, but that all should come to repentance' (2 Peter 3:9).

If God can find a person like Hagar, destitute and desperate in the desert, can't He just as easily find you or me, no matter how exiled we feel or what our separate wilderness experiences have been?

In John chapter 4 there is a story which we will examine in more detail later, of how Jesus spoke to a woman like Hagar who was sitting by a well, a Samaritan lady not considered part of the family of God. Yet Jesus singled this lady out and told her every last detail concerning her life, including how many husbands she'd had and what her current status was. Christ was interested in the personal details of her life. Religious background clearly wasn't an issue.

The same experience happened in the book of Joshua to Rahab, a harlot, who was excluded from God's people due to the fact that she was a Canaanite.

Yet, through the help of Rahab, God not only led the children of Israel safely into the Promised Land, He also saved Rahab, so vast and impartial is His love and compassion. Similarly, as the Egyptian slave girl Hagar reeled from the visitation of God's angel, surely the enormity of this fact must have dawned on her religious conscience. God's love reaches beyond the corridors of one church, one denomination, one skin colour and one social class. By sending His angel to her, God was demonstrating His great love, care and compassion for Hagar and for the world.

Psalm 91 speaks about the protecting power of angels and their function in our lives. The writer said: 'he shall give his angels charge over thee, to keep thee in all thy ways' (Psalm 91:11). While

Psalm 34 states: 'The angel of the LORD encamps all around those who fear Him, And delivers them' (Psalm 34:7, NKJV).

The angels are sent to those who fear God. The word 'fear' in this instance is the word 'reverence'. Therefore Hagar undoubtedly had a deep reverence and even respect for God in her heart. This is not as unusual as it may seem. There are many Christians who profess to follow God, but have an apparent lack of respect for God, while there are many people who do not profess to be a Christian, yet hold a deep reverence for the Almighty. How can this be? If you happen to be a Christian, I understand this rhetoric makes for uncomfortable reading, but this is sometimes the case and should challenge believers to truly worship the God they profess to serve.

Not once, but twice God sent angels to deliver Hagar out of all her troubles. What a challenge to true believers this is! After all, Psalm 91 begins with the words: 'He that dwells in the secret place of the most High shall abide under the shadow of the Almighty' (Psalm 91:1, JUB). In other words, God's children are promised daily protection and a safe eternal passage by the angels when they choose to fear (respect) and live close to God.

David Jeremiah wrote:

'What a loving God we serve! Not only has He prepared a heavenly dwelling for us, but His angels also accompany us as we transition from this world to the next.'[3]

Perhaps you have stopped abiding under the shadow of the Almighty. Maybe you are not living as close to God as you once did. It's not too late to address this. It's not too late to worship the Lord again in spirit and in truth. Being turned around by the angels of God before it's too late is a blessing and a mercy we should never take for granted from a loving and pardoning God. It is for our benefit and our own well-being. Angels are real! Angels do have a purpose! And the knowledge that angels are always watching over us, protecting us when we're in great peril here on earth or waiting to usher us to heaven's gates when we leave this scene of time, gives one great peace and much hope for the future.

Hagar responded to the words of the angel, then turned around and did what God had intended all along – her duty in the house of Abraham and Sarah.

For further thought, prayer and reflection

- Name some Bible characters God sent angels to how did these angels impact their lives?
- Do you believe in the ministry of angels? Do you believe they appear today, or do you think it was just in Bible days? What reasons do you have for believing/not believing?
- What is the purpose of angels, and why do they exist?
- Why would God send an angel to Hagar given that she was considered to be outside the covenant of God?
- Do you know anyone whose life has been impacted by the visitation of an angel? If yes, how has it changed their life?

Notes

1. azquotes.com.
2. shortstories101.com, entitled 'A tear to the eye', my paraphrase.
3. azquotes.com.

Thirteen:
Spring is Sprung

Spring is sprung, the grass is ris, I wonder where the birdies is;
they say the birds is on the wing, ain't that absurd? I always
thought the wing was on the bird. (Anon)

Picture the scene! Abraham and Sarah are conversing in their home. Suddenly, they hear familiar footsteps outside, a sound both of them would have recognised.

Maybe it was how she dragged her feet, or the way she rustled her long clothing over the dusty ground; or perhaps she possessed a silent grace immediately identifiable; nonetheless, Hagar's returning steps were unmistakable. Glancing at her husband, Sarah excitedly remarks: 'It's Hagar!'

As the tent door opened and her maidservant entered their dwelling, consider the expressions on the faces of the devastated couple. A person they concluded had left for good was back standing before them in their own home – just as if she'd never been away.

The woman who was carrying their son had mercifully returned and their plan to have a child was still a reality. The hopes and aspirations they'd carried for years were not impossible; nor had they gone up in smoke, after all.

For days, even weeks, poor Abraham and Sarah might well have assumed their dream of cradling their own child was over. During Hagar's absence, Sarah would have been kicking herself for pushing her maidservant over the edge, while Abraham would surely have lamented over the loss of the son he'd always longed for.

But with Hagar now back, ready to submit again to their authority, Abraham and Sarah must have been thrilled at the 'prodigal' daughter's return. Of course, they wouldn't have been best pleased at Hagar's absconding in the first place, but neither would Hagar have been amused at Sarah's mistreatment of her before she left. So, as uncomfortable as that day must have been for all of them, a partial truce emerged and everyone became a winner!

Circumstances appear to have improved noticeably thereafter. Ishmael was born, and there was no trace of any trouble in the family, until many years later when Ishmael experienced unexpected competition in the arrival of the promised son, Isaac – an event for which God had well prepared both Abraham and Sarah.

This is where things get very interesting, both from a domestic and spiritual point of view. The Bible states: 'And the LORD visited Sarah as he had said, and the LORD did unto Sarah as he had spoken. For Sarah conceived, and bare Abraham a son in his old age, at the set time of which God had spoken to him. And Abraham called the name of his son that was born unto him, whom Sarah bare to him, Isaac' (Genesis 21:1–3).

Similar to the birth of Christ, the birth of Isaac was miraculous and it came at God's set time. Abraham was 100 years old and Sarah, his wife, ninety years old when the birth actually occurred. Just when Abraham and Sarah least expected it, God gave them the desire of their hearts. Even when it didn't seem possible, all things proved possible with God!

To use that well-known phrase – spring had finally sprung!

The term 'spring is sprung' originates from a poem, often accredited to Ogden Nash, but the author is, in fact, the very famous poet, 'Anonymous'. The poem goes, as we have already read above: 'Spring is sprung, the grass is ris, I wonder where the birdies is; they say the birds is on the wing, ain't that absurd? I always thought the wing was on the bird.' It's generally associated with the arrival of the long-awaited season of spring; or anything long sought-after, for that matter. Translation of the rhyme into Standard English would read: 'Springtime has arrived and the grass has started to grow once more. I wonder where the birds are nesting. They say the birds are on the wing (flying). But that's absurd. It's the other way round; the wings are on the birds.' What do you do when something you had all-but given up on takes wings again? What happens when the thing you refused to wait for spectacularly appears when you least expect it? And how do you react when your dream turns up in completely different packaging to how you envisaged?

For years, Abraham, Sarah and Hagar may wrongly have assumed Ishmael was the promised son God had spoken to Abraham about. Abraham loved Ishmael and, undoubtedly, would have brought him up in the ways of the Lord, training him for great things and, who knows, it's conceivable that he even shared frequently with him how he was God's chosen son! How many times, for example, did Abraham teach him to pray and talk to him about godly things? Did he declare that Ishmael was the 'heir to his property' – holdings which were considerable, given Abraham's extreme wealth?

Ishmael might understandably have viewed himself as the 'prince in waiting'. He had no rivals at that stage of his life. He was without doubt excited and proud to be given the chance to succeed a man such as Abraham – somebody known to be a notable man of God.

Yet such a succession never actually took place. Why? The appointed birth of Isaac changed everything; a person the Bible says was God's original choice to continue the covenantal blessing of Abraham. God's promised son duly arrived, but not at the time or in the manner Abraham and Sarah ever imagined.

There is great confusion and misunderstanding regarding the birth of the promised son in the book of Genesis. For example, while Isaac was named as the promised son, in choosing Isaac, it's extremely important to point out how God had not in any way rejected Ishmael, whom He later made into a great nation.

Writing to the Galatians, Paul explains how Abraham was shown by God how the son produced by union with the bondwoman (Hagar) was born in the ordinary way, that is, according to the flesh, but Abraham's son by the free woman (Sarah) was born as the result of a promise (Galatians 4:23). The name Isaac means 'laughter'. His birth was a supernatural event – the product of Abraham and Sarah's waiting in trust upon the covenant blessings of the Lord. The birth of Ishmael was, on the other hand, an ordinary, natural conception. It was the result of the failure of Abraham and Sarah to trust in the Lord and to wait for His perfect will.

There was nothing supernatural in the birth of Ishmael at all, and the arrival of the baby Ishmael was therefore not auspicious.

Significantly, that didn't mean it was not an important birth in God's plan, and it's equally important to point out that nor did it mean God didn't love Ishmael.

Abraham and Ishmael were already circumcised. The covenantal blessing was already in place. No doubt Abraham, Sarah and even Hagar had well settled for the fact that Ishmael was the long-awaited promised son. Yet God threw a spanner into the works with the announcement to Abraham that he would have another son born to him, by Sarah – something Abraham and Sarah considered ridiculous.

For example, prior to the birth of Isaac, we read how God told Abraham that he and Sarah would have a son (Isaac) which caused Abraham to laugh at the thought of such a supernatural event – 'Then Abraham fell upon his face, and laughed, and said in his heart, Shall a child be born unto him that is an hundred years old? And shall Sarah, that is ninety years old, bear?' (Genesis 17:17).

On hearing this news, Sarah laughed, too! 'Therefore Sarah laughed within herself, saying, After I am waxed old shall I have pleasure, my lord being old also?' (Genesis 18:12). The name Isaac means 'laughter'. Later, Sarah declared, 'God has brought me laughter, and everyone who hears about this will laugh with me' (Genesis 21:6, NIV 1984).

This reaction of laughter is normal, of course. Even today when women have children well past the age of childbirth, people chuckle and are amazed at the event. It makes the front pages of newspapers and the top stories on our TV news bulletins.

But Abraham was 100 years old and his wife ninety! Isaac was indeed born, just as God had promised – in a supernatural way. Spring had sprung, leaving Abraham with a serious problem and teaching him and people of generations thereafter another significant lesson. God's promise doesn't always arrive in the way or at the time we expect, and neither are His plans for our lives straightforward.

Once Abraham became aware that Isaac was the promised son, not Ishmael, there was no turning back – he had to tell Ishmael. What a difficult task this would have been for Abraham. He loved Ishmael dearly and had prayed for his son many times.

Imagine Ishmael's and Hagar's pain when they realise Isaac is the 'main man', if you like. Imagine waking up one day and understanding you've not only been rejected by your earthly father, but you don't feel loved by your heavenly Father either. This would have been Ishmael's position.

Yet God had not rejected Ishmael. He loved him and had a great purpose for his life. God made a promise to Abraham that his offspring would be as the stars of the sky. (see Genesis 15:5). God willingly answered Abraham's prayers regarding Ishmael telling him: 'And as for Ishmael, I have heard you. Behold, I have blessed him, and will make him fruitful, and will multiply him exceedingly. He shall beget twelve princes, and I will make him a great nation' (Genesis 17:20, NKJV).

Indeed on three other occasions God went to great lengths to point out that Ishmael hadn't, in any way, been rejected – twice when he spoke to Hagar, and on another occasion when he spoke to Abraham. In His goodness, God acknowledged that Ishmael was Abraham's son and therefore he, too, would be blessed. True, Ishmael has been rejected by people ever since, even spiritual leaders, but not by God.

I am reminded of the fate of Jacob and Esau. By God's choice, His covenant blessings passed through Jacob, not Esau (even though Esau was the firstborn). It is normal for the older brother to inherit the father's blessing, but not in the case of Jacob and

Esau and Isaac and Ishmael. Here the younger becomes the main heir. Paul, writing to the Romans, said: 'The elder shall serve the younger' (Romans 9:12) – a reference to how the younger (Christianity) has replaced the elder (Judaism) as heir to the covenant. This does not, however, give Christian's free licence to act superior or hostile towards other religions.

In fact, regarding Esau and his descendants, Moses told the children of Israel 'Do not hate an Edomite (a descendant of Esau), for he is your brother' (Deuteronomy 23:7, NLV). In other words, the choice of Jacob did not mean the rejection of Esau, just as the choice of Isaac is not the rejection of Ishmael. Esau was given a blessing, just like Ishmael, not a rejection but, significantly, it was decidedly inferior to the covenant blessing pronounced on Jacob. Consequently, in the book of Romans, Paul shows how God chose to bless Jacob over Esau, as He blessed Isaac over Ishmael. But wait a minute! Doesn't Malachi 1:1–3 record how God loved Jacob and hated Esau? That's true and many Christians are understandably confused when they read Romans 9:13: 'As it is written: "Jacob have I loved, but Esau have I hated."' The question which follows this is obvious: Can the God of love hate people? This verse, coupled with the rest of Romans 9, has led many to believe that God doesn't love everyone, at least with regard to their eternal salvation. Instead, He seems to randomly select some people for salvation and some people for damnation. But is this correct?

Once we understand that God was not referring to individual salvation in these verses, but Israel's national role in redemptive history, the answer is 'no'.

Paul is actually quoting from Malachi 1, 2 and 3 and by using the word 'Jacob' to refer to the nation of Israel and the word 'Esau' to refer to the nation of Edom it follows that He was not speaking about Jacob and Esau as individuals, but as nations.

It also naturally follows that Romans 9, 10 and 11 are all about national Israel and her role in redemptive history. Romans 9 refers to Israel's past, Romans 10 refers to her present, and Romans 11 refers to her future.

It is theologically incorrect therefore to interpret Romans 9 to be referring to an individual's salvation. Such thinking can lead to extreme prejudice. Not every individual in Israel was elected to be saved. 'For not all who are descended from Israel belong to Israel.' (Romans 9:6, ESV)

God has always used nations to accomplish His purpose, just as He works through individuals. Israel may well have been the chosen nation to bring forth the Messiah, yet that didn't mean every Israelite would be individually saved. Salvation is not, and never has been, based on a person's nationality. Finally, it is vital to highlight that the word 'hate' used in in Malachi 1 is a Hebrew expression which actually means to 'love less'. For example in Genesis 29:30 the phrase 'loved Rachel more than Leah' (ESV) actually means Leah was hated. God does not therefore hate any individuals, but he does bless some nations more than others.

Let us remember Ishmael and his mother, Hagar, were human beings. Ishmael can be forgiven for feeling betrayed, having been convinced for all those years that he would be the awaited one – the promised son. A backlash was probably inevitable and it duly came from Ishmael himself. The worm had turned and the course of history was set. Those deep, former wounds which Hagar received, wounds which had once forced her into the wilderness while pregnant with Ishmael many years previously, also resurfaced within her. So, too, did the sin of jealousy within

Ishmael who suddenly displayed the spirit of Joseph's brothers and began to mock his younger, more favoured brother.

When Abraham held a banquet to celebrate the weaning of his new son, Isaac, his older brother Ishmael began to mock and persecute his younger brother to such an extent his mother, Sarah, stepped in. As the steady stream of insults and frequent taunts towards Isaac increased and possibly daily persecution of Isaac intensified, things came to a head for Sarah who simply refused to sit back and watch her son being abused by his older brother.

Suddenly the shoe was on the other foot, so to speak! Now Sarah and her son, Isaac, were the victims in the house – they were the ones being oppressed – not Hagar or Ishmael. In Sarah's world, it was time for Hagar and Ishmael to leave Canaan, time for Ishmael to spread his wings – and time for Isaac to take centre stage and to grow and flourish in their home as God's promised son.

We hear a lot about religious discrimination and racial intolerance today as though it's a recent occurrence, yet religious bias and bullying dates right back to this historic feud between Isaac's parents and Ishmael's mother.

Sarah's way of handing the persecution of her son, Isaac, of course, was to suggest casting Hagar and Ishmael out of the house altogether. A quite merciless measure, on the face of it, but that's how the Bible describes it. Sarah said to Abraham: 'Drive out this maid and her son, for the son of this maid shall not be an heir with my son Isaac' (Genesis 21:10, NASB). The New Living Translation of this verse reads: 'So she turned to Abraham and demanded, "Get rid of that slave woman and her son. He is not going to share the inheritance with my son, Isaac. I won't have it!"'

It's amazing what people will do to a fellow human being when they are convinced God is on their side – Abraham and Sarah were no exception. Sarah is so enraged she doesn't even use

Hagar's name, preferring the derogatory term of 'slave woman'.

Abraham and Sarah may not have displayed the same brutality as some groups today who harm, murder and destroy in the name of God, but they evidently lacked mercy, feeling and compassion for two relatives who had shared their home for many years. We cannot overlook this strange irony, given the fact that both served the living God. It is more than a paradox. It is almost a contradiction!

With ruthless efficiency, Sarah was not restrained in drawing attention to Hagar's and Ishmael's position, both ethnically and spiritually and, despite the many years of fellowship and friendship with them, she was quite prepared to have them expelled from her home.

Sarah wanted Abraham to exercise what we refer to today as 'tough love'. In Sarah's view, there was no room for a 'heathen boy' like Ishmael who was causing continual strife and dissension in their home. Interestingly the very same spirit remains today – it's called 'spiritual elitism' or 'racism within the church', and it's more common than we might imagine. Spiritual pride is the reason behind much suffering in the world today.

As we shall see in the following chapters, Hagar and Ishmael were eventually forfeited; cast out of the house indefinitely. Thereafter peace returned to the home but, not surprisingly, the family became more fractured than ever before. True, Isaac was protected, but at a huge price. He was left estranged from his half-brother. The decision to remove Hagar and Ishmael by Sarah and Abraham would separate brethren for centuries to come and turn them into total strangers.

Abraham and Sarah had won the battle, but given events since, hardly the war!

For further thought, prayer and reflection

- How do you think you might react if God gave you the thing you have been praying about for years?
- What was the difference in the birth of Ishmael and Isaac? Why did Ishmael never become the promised son?
- Did the choice of Isaac as the promised son mean Ishmael was rejected by God?
- When God said He hated Esau, what did He mean by this?
- Following Sarah's decision, what have been the theological consequences for our world today?

Fourteen:
Whose Side is God On?

I do not boast that God is on my side, I humbly pray that I am on God's side.
(Abraham Lincoln)[1]

Are you thinking what I'm thinking? Is it possible that a loving and compassionate God would endorse the ruthless removal of Hagar and her son by Abraham and Sarah from their home?

As Abraham anguished over the eviction of his second wife and son, the Bible records how God told him not to mourn, but to listen to the words of his wife, because everything would be OK: 'And God said unto Abraham, Let it not be grievous in thy sight because of the lad, and because of thy bondwoman; in all that Sarah hath said unto thee, hearken unto her voice; for in Isaac shall thy seed be called. And also of the son of the bondwoman will I make a nation, because he is thy seed' (Genesis 21:12–13). Even in our comparative darkness and limited understanding, we still have an inbuilt conscience which helps us differentiate between right and wrong, good and evil, justice and injustice. So, in terms of even-handedness, this attempt by Sarah to evict Hagar and Ishmael from her home does seem hard to fathom.

Nevertheless, God always performs what's best for us because He's working things out for our eternal benefit, not necessarily for our immediate benefit. Even when we can't see it, His justice is perfect and His love far greater than we can ever possibly comprehend.

For example, had Ishmael remained in the house it would have been a torturous time for Isaac, who would have ended up physically and spiritually ruined by the persecution of his older brother, while God already had a destiny and plan for both Ishmael and Hagar. Yes, a precarious path lay ahead for both, but a path that would ultimately lead to the purpose of Ishmael's life and, in the process, draw Hagar closer to God.

Of course, Hagar would not have realised that God was in the midst of her distress. Surely, she must have thought to herself, this wasn't the justice or the fairness of a benevolent God. She might, with some justification, have felt God's disapproval of her and asked herself many times just what she had done wrong. Didn't Abraham preach to Hagar and others about the faithfulness of God? Hagar had tried to be faithful to Abraham and caused him no real trouble. What honour would there be in wandering about the wilderness of Beersheba as a single parent with no identity, no home and no provision for her journey? Some honour there!

Confused and angry, Hagar must have wondered why, years previously, God had sent her back to Canaan to finally give birth to Ishmael. The angel came and stood before her. It couldn't have been clearer. God had privileged Hagar with an angelic visitation, so how had things come to this? She had followed his instructions to the letter, but where was God in this sorry mess now?

Hagar's situation is similar to Joseph's, a man who served God with a pure heart, but was sold into Egypt by his brothers, and imprisoned. At first Joseph didn't understand any of it. Only years later, when his brothers turned up in Egypt and sought his forgiveness, did Joseph recall his childhood dreams which gave him a vision of his brothers one day bowing before him. This caused Joseph to reply to his brothers: 'But as for you, ye thought evil against me; but God meant it unto good, to bring to pass, as it is this day, to save many people alive' (Genesis 50:20). The CEV version reads: 'You tried to harm me, but God made it turn out for the best, so that he could save all these people, as he is now doing.'

Have you ever believed you did the right thing, but still ended up with the wrong result? Have you ever been convinced God was on your side, only to experience that He wasn't? Do you realise that God can still bring good out of what may be perceived by you as a bad situation?

As Hagar and Ishmael faced the reality of those final hours in Abraham and Sarah's abode, I can just picture her asking the obvious question: Whose side is God on, anyway?

From both a human and spiritual perspective, it certainly appeared that God was on the side of Abraham and Sarah, not Hagar and Ishmael. For example, Isaac was already announced as the promised son and, while Abraham and Sarah were secure in Canaan, poor Hagar was about to embark on a second spell in the wilderness with no guarantee of any future blessings. The drudgery which lay ahead was unthinkable!

But hold on! Hadn't she been visited by an angel? Surely God was on her side, not Abraham's or Sarah's side. Notwithstanding, there was a key difference between Abraham, Sarah and Hagar. The former had already made the decision to follow the one true God – Jehovah – the latter, on the other hand, was an Egyptian and a follower of a pagan faith, yet through her struggles, Abraham and Sarah's God was continually revealing Himself to her, urging her ever closer to conversion.

Through her experiences in the wilderness, Hagar would discover something precious – something all of us must come to understand – God doesn't take sides! Why? He loves all of His creation equally, and He loves people from every background.

Remember, Moses stood at the gate of the camp and announced: 'Who is on the Lord's side? let him come unto me' (Exodus 32:26). Significantly he didn't say 'Whose side is the Lord on?' In other words, God gives us a choice to reject or accept Him. Joshua said: 'choose you this day whom ye will serve ... as for me and my house, we will serve the LORD' (Joshua 24:15).

Notice the emphasis is towards what we do, not on what God has already done.

Rather than ask: Whose side is God on? A better question therefore is: Are we on God's side?

Notwithstanding, how many Christians have invented a god they believe is on their side? Throughout history, we have witnessed people carrying out some atrocious deeds while brazenly claiming that God was on their side. But saying we are a Christian doesn't guarantee that God is 'on our side' any more than being an ancient Israelite suggested that God was on theirs. Paul the apostle stated: 'not all who are descended from Israel are Israel' (Romans 9:6, NIV 1984) – a reference to the fact that it is not the natural children who are God's children, but it is the children of the promise (Isaac) who are regarded as Abraham's true offspring.

God is not on the side of those who insist on convincing God and others that their way is right. He's not on the side of Islamic extremists who murder and maim in the name of God. He's not on the side of the Christian extremist who refuses to love people just because they are different to him. He's not on the side of anyone who presents an unloving God.

How many churches and denominations, for example, have separated due to claiming God is on their side? Spiritual pride and a naive notion that 'God was on their side' has caused more church splits, disunity and fractured relationships than any just cause.

During the American Civil War, Abraham Lincoln was asked if God was on his side. His reply is most humbling: 'I do not boast that God is on my side, I humbly pray that I am on God's side.'[2]

These days, as the entire world takes sides in the ongoing Arab-Israeli conflict, it's worth recalling the mighty soldier Joshua's experience in relation to just whose side God is on.

The Bible states: 'Now when Joshua was near Jericho, he looked up and saw a man standing in front of him with a drawn sword in his hand. Joshua went up to him and asked, "Are you for us or for our enemies?" "Neither," he replied, "but as commander of the army of the LORD I have now come"' (Joshua 5:13,14, NIV 1984). That must have been quite a shock to Joshua's spiritual pride and religious preconceived notions. God had sent help, but told Joshua that He wasn't on one side or the other. In fact, God's answer to Joshua's question about whose side the angel was on was quite philosophical; in effect, God says to Joshua: 'Whether I am on your side is not the real issue. The most important question, Joshua, is whether you and Israel are on my side.'

There can be no more life-changing trial than finding yourself on the other side, but , when we begin to feel such empathy and compassion for those in the 'opposite camp', God is clearly doing a work of grace in our hearts.

The man Joshua saw was the commander of the armies of Yahweh, and notice how he didn't fight on either side against the other. Instead, he had his own agenda, to command the will and purpose of God in the coming battle. Too often people view religion as an 'us' and 'them' situation – Christians fighting Muslims, Muslims fighting Christians, Muslims opposing Jews, and Jews opposing Muslims – and we know there are other religious disputes of similar nature today.

In the same way, when God chose Isaac over Ishmael as the promised son, He wasn't taking sides. He simply had another plan for Ishmael's life. God loved both boys and blessed them in different ways. He had a path, a destiny and life for both of them. Similarly today, I do not believe the Lord takes sides in a human sense, and neither must we, if we are to leave the door open for people of all faiths to accept Jesus.

It's amazing how people go out of their way to convince others that their cause is godly and fully endorsed by God Himself. Indeed, have you noticed how many individual Christians and combined organisations assume that God is exclusively on their side? God is with them and their private sect and no one else! They say things like: 'Our church is the only church!'; 'Our denomination is the only denomination!'; 'Our doctrine is the only true doctrine!' This ludicrous line of thinking has even reached the stage where some Christians believe God is a supporter of their local football team or current political party. While this may sound almost humorous, spiritual ignorance is no laughing matter. Outrageously I've even heard some militant Christian preachers warn: 'Oppose me and God will curse and destroy you and your family!' This is spiritual abuse of the highest order and extreme spiritual pride to boot!

God is not a destroyer; He's a restorer!

We must seek again the heart of God in order for all people groups to be saved. Spiritual elitism leads to our own 'small gods' and the building of our own 'miniature kingdoms' which we have devised. Rather than praying according to God's agenda and with His heart of love for a broken world, 'doing our own thing' and boasting how God is the architect behind it all only creates more division and sectarian strife.

Joshua adds a very meaningful question in this passage, namely: 'What does my Lord say to His servant?' (Joshua 5:14, NKJV). Isn't this a most sobering thought? For example, do we listen to what the Lord is saying? Do we consider what God truly wants, or do we follow 'fleshly desires' and our own deep-rooted spiritual conceit and private prejudices?

Instead of jumping into a situation with the presumption that God is on our side, it's imperative that we are on His. Better to walk in step with His Spirit than to follow the agenda of the crowd, the church, or even misguided spiritual leaders.

How many Christians, for example, are aware that countless Muslims, who are being rejected by other faiths, are accepted by God? Many Muslims are testifying to how God has sent angels to their homes and districts to reveal the one true God – Jesus Christ. This is happening regularly today. Without the help of any human form of evangelism, numerous Muslims and even people of other faiths are being converted to Christ, having received a personal visitation from God's heavenly messengers.

Christianity Today reported in April 2014 how Muslims are

now leading other Muslims to Christ. In his book entitled *A Wind in the House of Islam*,[3] David Garrison, who has interviewed thousands of Muslims, confirms this. One Muslim man in Iran had the same dream three nights consecutively about Christ, leading him to conclude that Jesus Christ is the only true God. Why would God choose to visit Muslims and people of other religions in this way? For the same reason He not once, but twice sent an angel to rescue an Egyptian slave girl called Hagar. God is not on any particular side. He's no respecter of persons and His love is incomprehensible. He has no prejudice and He desires for us to be on His side.

Greg Albrecht wrote in *Whose Side is God On?*:

God is on the side of our next-door neighbours whose dogs bark and bother us, the neighbours who never mow their lawn and who have loud parties. He's on the side of people who don't attend your church – or people who don't attend any church – or people who are not even Christians. God's love is big enough – there's enough of it to go around, even for people who don't even believe in Him – at least not yet. Whose side is God on? He's on the side of people who live outside of our borders and boundaries, who speak languages we don't understand and practice and love a culture we don't know or appreciate. God does not take sides as humans do. He is not against anyone. He doesn't have favourites. The real question for you and me is whether we are on God's side. [4]

If our hearts are only to see people from our own family, district, church, or religious background saved, or to see people of our own skin colour or culture redeemed, then this is falling short of God's vast plan of salvation for the world.

Much prayer is now required regarding the current suffering experienced by Israelis and Palestinians, Muslims and Christians, Jews and Arabs. We must pray that out of this chaos, evil and violence, many will be led to faith in the Prince of Peace, Jesus Christ.

What has all of this got to do with Hagar? I believe Hagar would have felt the same rejection and isolation that many Muslims and people of other religions feel today, after her expulsion from the home of Abraham and Sarah. She, too, must have felt like a castaway. Despised and alienated, she wandered through a wilderness of sheer loneliness and isolation. She would have assumed God was with 'them' – Abraham and Sarah – and not with her and Ishmael. All she could see was how God had blessed Abraham and Sarah and given them what the Bible describes as 'The blessing of the Lord makes one rich, And He adds no sorrow with it' (Proverbs 10:22, NKJV).

Think about it! They had the promised son, just like God had pledged. They had plenty of supplies. They had a home and family of their own. They had a good name in the community. They had God's approval, and yet poor Hagar was left to wander in the wilderness without any of those blessings.

It's one thing to feel abandoned by God's people, but when you're out there, in the cold light of day, a nomad, wandering about with your faith destroyed and your dreams in tatters, it's an altogether different thing to feel rejected by God Himself. The natural reaction at such a time is to turn away from God and His people. The fact is, God hadn't rejected Hagar at all and, if you happen to be in a similar place, He hasn't rejected you. On the contrary, He has promised never to leave or forsake you (Hebrews 13:5). Even if God's people have rejected you, and no doubt this has impaired your faith, know that God isn't finished with you – not by a long, long way.

For further thought, prayer and reflection

- Do you believe God endorsed the removal of both Hagar and Ishmael from the home of Abraham and Sarah? If so, why did He allow this event to happen to them?
- Do you have any human sympathy for Hagar and Ishmael? Do you have any sympathy for Abraham and Sarah?
- Have you ever believed you did the right thing but ended up with the wrong result?
- Whose side do you believe God is on?
- Does saying we are a Christian guarantee that God is on our side?
- Why is God saving Muslims and people of all religions around the world today?
- Do you have a heart to reach people for Jesus beyond your own community, culture or church group?

Notes

1. azquotes.com.
2. azquotes.com.
3. David Garrison, *A Wind in the House of Islam* (Monument, CO: WIGTake Resources, LLC, 2014).
4. floydandsally.com.

Fifteen:
Left to Die

No wickedness so distresses the believer as that which he witnesses in those who profess to be of the church of God.[1]

His eyes staring directly into Hagar's, righteous Abraham's words must have cut like a razor-sharp knife: 'Sarah and I have talked things over, Hagar; we would like you and Ishmael to leave the home, and there will be little provision for your journey.' Hagar and Ishmael's long stay in the home of Abraham and Sarah had come to an abrupt end. Shocked enough at the prospect of having to leave the only household they had, Hagar and Ishmael would certainly have been justified in expecting better support, but that wasn't to be.

In those days, of course, there was no such thing as child maintenance or matrimonial compensation. Just as well, perhaps, because old Abraham had no intention of paying anything to his wife Hagar, despite her years of service as a maidservant to the home in Canaan they shared with his first wife, Sarah.

Regarding this insensitive separation the Bible states: 'And Abraham rose up early in the morning, and took bread, and a bottle of water, and gave it unto Hagar, putting it on her shoulder, and the child, and sent her away: and she departed, and wandered in the wilderness of Beersheba' (Genesis 21:14).

It's the 'and sent her away' which is so hard to comprehend, isn't it?

Hagar must have felt gutted that all her years of assistance and obedience to the Abraham name and family circle had stood for nothing; devastated that her own husband and his first wife, Sarah, could so easily dispense with her services.

Remember, having given birth to Ishmael, Hagar had only done as she was asked when Sarah, unable to give birth, approached Hagar for help. Nevertheless, Hagar and her son were left to die by Abraham… left to die by his wife Sarah… and, left to die, by of all people, God's people!

Hagar appeared to be a cooperative maidservant to Abraham and Sarah. True, she got a little too puffed up when she imagined Ishmael as Abraham's successor, but what woman wouldn't have, given her precarious position? In truth, she'd probably been 'too loyal' to a couple she may well have viewed as having very short memories and being extremely heartless in their decision-making.

Hagar must have felt these two people didn't deserve the years of faithfulness and loyalty she'd given them. Abraham and Sarah believed they were working to God's instructions, 'God was on their side', as they saw it, but from a human standpoint that would have meant nothing to Hagar and her son at that time. On the contrary, as she left with just a bottle of water and a loaf of bread for her journey, not even sure of where she was going, Hagar must have regretted with all of her heart the day she returned to that same dwelling a few years previously. She must have rued the fact that she didn't continue down the road to Shur and begin a new life back in Egypt instead. Hagar must have thoroughly deplored every anxious step she took back towards Canaan.

Hagar had faithfully obeyed the voice of God and the angel when she followed God's leading. Why Abraham and Sarah were not more considerate of the sacrifice she'd made for their home and family is something which surely must have stuck in her throat. How could Sarah, and especially Abraham, her husband and father of their child, just leave her and Ishmael with no support? It was as if they had never existed!

Over the years, no doubt, Abraham and Sarah had told Hagar that their home was her home and their people her people. She believed she was part of the family and assumed she would grow old in that household and even die there. Perplexed as to how to inform Hagar that she was no longer wanted, I wonder what sort of excuses Abraham and Sarah might have dreamed up:

'We're so sorry, Hagar, but it's come to our attention that due to new legislation regarding slaves and their masters, it's no longer legal for you to reside in the home with us.'

'Besides, our son Isaac isn't happy with you and Ishmael living here, so there's really nothing more we can do for you.'

Picture Hagar lying awake at night, filled with anxiety at the thought of being removed from the only home she and her young son had. How would she cope? Hagar must have been shocked, hurt and stunned by such a development.

We have to bear in mind that it wasn't a stranger doing this, but people she had grown to trust and perhaps love. Granted, as Sarah's maidservant and being a slave, she would have been expected to do as she was asked – even in relation to sleeping with Abraham when Sarah couldn't give birth – but it is still feasible that love played some part in the act of devotion she displayed towards Abraham and Sarah. To therefore be abandoned, that kindness forgotten, and left to die, would have been a cruel blow to Hagar.

I still recall the story of a young man who was attacked by members of his own family because they were angry after he had left the family business they shared together. Over the years, he'd continually tried to win their affection, but was instead constantly rejected by his siblings, and especially so by his father – a ruthless man full of ambition and pride. This oppression led to the boy suffering a great deal of domestic intimidation, until one day, an incident occurred which left the young man so traumatised he felt he'd no alternative but to leave the family home also. After explaining his position to his father and brethren, he then said his goodbyes and reluctantly set off into the unknown.

Not long after his exit, however, his father and brothers were incensed and plotted to have him killed. They were furious at his leaving and weren't about to allow him to get away with it. Unthinkably, they waited for the right moment before attacking their brother with such ferocity that he almost died. They stamped on his head and gave him such a prolific beating, his face and body became almost unrecognisable. Incredibly, it wasn't strangers inflicting this harm to the man, but members of his own family. As their brother lay unconscious, with blood streaming out of him, remarkably they left the scene of violence, washed their hands and continued as though nothing had ever taken place.

Equally shocking was the fact that not once, following this deplorable incident, did they enquire after their brother or ask whether he was dead or alive. Instead, these malicious men carried on with their lives, oblivious to the suffering their brother endured and with no regard for the lengthy and painstaking rehabilitation period it took for their brother to make a full recovery.

In their uncontrolled rage, they had left their brother to die, and the only question the young man could ask when he later regained consciousness was – why? 'Why would people from my own family try to destroy me in such a ruthless and uncompassionate way?

In the same way, Hagar would have been left devastated and distressed by the actions of her so-called friends and family, Abraham and Sarah. In fact, Hagar and Ishmael's story is just one example of how some of the most painful wounds we receive are sometimes inflicted by the most unlikely people – our family, friends and even God's chosen vessels!

These wounds are not the same as wounds caused by others, even the wounds of an enemy. We can't write them off as spur of the moment mistakes. They are profoundly personal. These pains have been triggered by people who we're familiar with; by individuals we assumed loved and respected us.

When we receive such wounds it's heartbreaking. Being wounded in this way can be a very traumatic experience, the pain of which should never be underestimated. I believe there are many wounded people in the world today, and far too many wounded Christians.

Matthew Henry says: 'No wickedness so distresses the believer, as that which he witnesses in those who profess to be of the church of God.²

Perhaps you've experienced rejection, hurt, betrayal, or racial exclusion. Has the colour of your skin, your spiritual upbringing, your theological views or, some other issue, brought estrangement and disappointment from the place you least expected – your family, friends, or even the church you attended so faithfully? Instead of finding encouragement within the people of God, you've experienced persecution, and even segregation.

Then please understand you're not alone. The Bible not only records how Hagar and Ishmael were rejected by two of God's chosen people, it offers many similar accounts of how distinguished children of God were also abandoned and left to die by their nearest and dearest.

Before becoming Prime Minister of Egypt, for example, Joseph's principal hurts were caused mainly by his own brothers and closest family members who left him to die in a pit. Prior to becoming king, David was hounded by his ally, Saul. Jesus, too, endured betrayal by his closest friends, causing Him to declare – 'a man's enemies will be those of his own household' (Matthew 10:36, NKJV). In other words: 'A man's enemies will be inside his own front room.'

Often we come to understand that while Christ is a safe place, the church, or what we call home, can be anything but a safe place. Ann Graham Lotz records in *Wounded by God's People*: 'The "world" of Egypt seems safer than the "church" of Abraham's tent.'[3]

Being betrayed by friends and especially brethren can be a most traumatic experience. We can't get our heads around how those who profess to love us can so easily cast us aside. The psalmist records: 'For it was not an enemy that reproached me; then I could have borne it: neither was it he that hated me that did magnify himself against me; then I would have hid myself from him: But it was thou, a man mine equal, my guide, and mine acquaintance. We took sweet counsel together, and walked unto the house of God in company' (Psalm 55:12–14).

Abraham was widely known as the 'friend of God', but in this one ruthless act he proved to be no friend to Hagar or her son. Remember, Abraham was a man who was seen as an upright, righteous man.

Nevertheless, privately he and his wife, Sarah, turned their backs on the two people who needed their help the most. Why would Abraham and Sarah do such a cruel thing to people who'd become such a huge part of their family?

Did Abraham and Sarah also feel betrayed by Ishmael's mocking of Isaac? Were they constantly not happy with Hagar's presence because she was an Egyptian, and, saw Ishmael's behaviour as the opportunity to cast her and her son out of their home?

This doesn't, of course, excuse their actions, but people are people and don't always show the love and kindness they ought to.

In the epic movie *Ben-Hur*, Judah Ben-Hur (Charlton Heston) is betrayed by his best friend, the Roman leader Messala (Stephen Boyd). After Messala imprisons his friend and mother and sister, Judah Ben-Hur sobs loudly and cries: 'Is it possible Messala, is it possible you could do this to us, to people you've known, to a family you've loved?'[4]

Today we are not shocked by the behaviour of Messala, or two Old Testament believers like Abraham and Sarah; saddened, yes, but not surprised, because many of us have behaved in the same way, and many of us have also woefully borne the brunt of similar harsh treatment by those who had claimed to love us.

What am I saying? Hagar and Ishmael's story is actually not that unusual. Perhaps you are a person or even a professing Christian who has been 'left to die' by your closest allies. Unfortunately, cruelty by Christians against their own brethren happens all too often and, yes, even Jesus experienced this form of rejection. The Bible says that Christ, too, 'came unto his own, and his own received him not' (John 1:11) – a reference to how His own Jewish brethren rejected Him.

While it's hard to imagine two of God's chosen vessels – Abraham and Sarah – behaving in such an inconsiderate fashion, the same spirit is evident throughout the world today. Faithful people, who have given everything for the cause and cooperated in every way possible, are often cast aside and spurned by ungrateful employers, by family members, by friends and, more unpardonably, even by hard-hearted and insensitive church leaders.

This kind of rejection by one's own has seen many Christians flee from the church. It has resulted in countless people becoming scattered and without a place of worship.

Today we hear much about persecution of Christians around the world by other faiths, especially by Islamic extremists, and this is undoubtedly a grievous state of affairs which must be taken seriously and prayed much about; nevertheless, the persecution of Christians by other Christians can also become equally damaging to those who seek to continue to follow God. Persecution by one Christian against another is the 'elephant in the room' no one wants to talk about. Many people draw back from God because of horrendous treatment they experienced at church. This is wrong! I have constantly heard it said: 'There is no army in the world more proficient at burying their wounded than the Christian army.' How sad this is!

Just like the story of Joseph, who was left to die by his own flesh and blood, there are far too many accounts today of Christians who have been practically destroyed by their own brethren. As James the apostle wrote: 'My brethren, these things ought not so to be' (James 3:10), yet they are so, and this matter needs to be addressed.

God's Word commands us to love one another even as God has loved us. 'If a man say, I love God, and hateth his brother, he is a liar: for he that loveth not his brother whom he hath seen, how can he love God whom he hath not seen?' (1 John 4:20).

Peter says: 'And above all things have fervent [love] among yourselves: for [love] shall cover the multitude of sins' (1 Peter 4:8).

It's not just Christians, of course, who have been 'left to die' by other Christians. People of all religions and backgrounds are today experiencing surprising rejection by their families, friends, and even governments. There is a distinct lack of tolerance and acceptance. This has resulted in the deplorable development of millions of bereft and forgotten refugees and the rise of another global epidemic which has spiralled out of control – that of destitution or homelessness.

For further thought, prayer and reflection

- Have you ever been abandoned at a time when you needed help the most by family, friends, or even by God's people? How has this made you feel? Has it prevented you from growing in your relationship with God? Have you blamed God for this setback, or do you accept that people have been the problem? Do you feel any responsibility yourself?

- Do you know any Christians who have been badly wounded by other believers? Is there something you can do to help restore these people?

Notes

1. Matthew Henry's Concise Commentary, biblehub.com.
2. Matthew Henry's Concise Commentary, biblehub.com.
3. Anne Graham Lotz, *Wounded by God's People* (London: Hodder & Stoughton, 2013).
4. From the movie *Ben-Hur*, quotation appearing on imdb.com.

Sixteen:
Nowhere to Lay Her Head

Feed the hungry, clothe the naked, forgive the guilty, welcome the unwanted, care for the ill, love your enemies and do unto others as you would have them do unto you.
(Steve Maraboli)[1]

Hagar's homeless plight began in the wilderness of Paran, northern Arabia, and is thought to have ended with the building of the city of Mecca – a place later known as the centre for Islamic religion – after Ishmael had become the father of the Arab nations.

What happened prior to this more settled period in their lives, however, is actually quite unthinkable. Hagar and her son would have been viewed by any Arab Egyptian traders as two refugees wandering without a home, bereft of food and even water. The wilderness of Paran was a barren place and, with no real provision supplied by Abraham before they left Canaan, inevitably it would not be long before Hagar would encounter not just hard times, but a 'make or break' situation.

Without shelter, food or water, just how would Hagar and her teenage son survive? To say Hagar desperately needed help, support and even some supernatural intervention is no exaggeration.

Their story is similar to the tale of a man and his wife who'd fallen on hard times during the midst of the world recession. After they were unexpectedly removed from their home, they spent the first night sleeping in their car in a local car park. They were in such financial trouble that the man had to make a decision between using his engine for heat or turning the engine off in order to save petrol. It was 1 a.m. and the couple's sense of distress was understandable, At that precise moment, however, another car pulled up beside them. It was the familiar face of a friend they had once attended church with. At first the conversation was awkward, as the couple tried to pretend they were just having a late night out. The man wasn't convinced and asked was everything OK. At this point the lady in the car began to sob, and when their friend discerned that they had nowhere to lay their heads, he realised the seriousness of their situation. Immediately the compassion of God kicked in and he brought them home, put them up for several months and even fed and clothed them, until they got back on their feet.

What am I saying? Their friend was a true friend! He sacrificed his own space to show the love of God to two people who had lost everything and didn't know where to turn.

There are many homeless people in our world today; and just like this this man and his wife and, in the same way, Hagar and Ishmael, bereft in the wilderness, these people require assistance. At such times, the arrival of human support can be a Godsend – no matter where it comes from. Many people have been criticised for making room in their homes in order to help facilitate refugees, yet such gracious hospitality can, for many people, often prove the difference between death and survival". How can we criticise such a merciful and kind action?

I wonder, did anyone offer to help Hagar and Ishmael during their initial exile in the wilderness? Did anyone offer to put them up and feed them or clothe them? True, the wilderness was a sparse area, but surely they would have met someone, and what was that someone's reaction? Were they filled with the compassion of God, and equally willing to meet their needs? There is no record of Hagar or Ishmael getting any human support; instead, God supernaturally provided for them. Notwithstanding, their situation raises an interesting and thought-provoking point – does God expect us to love and care for our fellow human beings, especially the homeless and the destitute within our own society? Steve Maraboli wrote: 'Feed the hungry, clothe the naked, forgive the guilty, welcome the unwanted, care for the ill, love your enemies and do unto others as you would have them do unto you.'

On 24 May 2015, the Belfast Telegraph newspaper in Northern Ireland carried a very moving description of how a well-known radio presenter came to the rescue of a local DJ who had found himself living rough on the freezing streets of Belfast.

The presenter was walking past this man one evening when he stopped and then lay down on the ground beside him, asking him why he was living rough. Following an emotional encounter, the big-hearted radio star picked the man up and took him to one of Belfast's top hotels and unselfishly paid for his stay there until the homeless man got his life back on track. He even followed up on the progress of the man to ensure he had made a full recovery. The BBC presenter, renowned for his no-nonsense questioning of local politicians, performed this great act of human kindness when he voluntarily went out on the streets of Belfast just a few days before Christmas in 2013 with volunteers from a charity that helps the homeless.

This caring gesture reminded me of a story Jesus once told about the Good Samaritan. The Bible records:

And, behold, a certain lawyer stood up, and tempted him, saying, Master, what shall I do to inherit eternal life? He said unto him, What is written in the law? how readest thou? And he answering said, Thou shalt love the Lord thy God with all thy heart, and with all thy soul, and with all thy strength, and with all thy mind; and thy neighbour as thyself. And he said unto him, Thou hast answered right: this do, and thou shalt live. But he, willing to justify himself, said unto Jesus, And who is my neighbour? And Jesus answering said, A certain man went down from Jerusalem to Jericho, and fell among thieves, which stripped him of his raiment, and wounded him, and departed, leaving him half dead. And by chance there came down a certain priest that way: and when he saw him, he passed by on the other side. And likewise a Levite, when he was at the place, came and looked on him, and passed by on the other side. But a certain Samaritan, as he journeyed, came where he was: and when he saw him, he had compassion on him, And went to him, and bound up his wounds, pouring in oil and wine, and set him on his own beast, and brought him to an inn, and took care of him. And on the morrow when he departed, he took out two pence, and gave them to the host, and said unto him, Take care of him; and whatsoever thou spendest more, when I come again, I will repay thee. Which now of these three, thinkest thou, was neighbour unto him that fell among the thieves? And he said, He that shewed mercy on him. Then said Jesus unto him, Go, and do thou likewise. (Luke 10:25–37)

The application from Jesus in this parable is obvious: actions speak louder than words, and people who profess to follow the God of love are often too busy or too selfish to stop and help their homeless neighbour. Remembering the homeless in prayer is good; giving them shelter and feeding their bellies is better! Homeless people don't only require our prayers, they need urgent assistance and God's love and care.

For a variety of reasons, a multitude of people from various backgrounds are currently without a roof over their heads, but Jesus understands their pain. During His earthly ministry, Christ was told by a would-be disciple, 'Lord, I will follow You wherever You go' (Luke 9:57, NKJV); to which he replied, 'Foxes have holes and birds of the air have nests, but the Son of Man has nowhere to lay His head' (Luke 9:58, NKJV). He has been where homeless people are and identifies with every aspect of our humanity. Not only was He homeless, however, Jesus too was a refugee, having had to flee from Egypt. Even in his childhood we see that Jesus was made homeless and became in great danger. The Bible says in Matthew 2:12–15: 'Now when they had gone, an angel of the Lord appeared to Joseph in a dream and said, "Get up! Take the Child and His mother and flee to Egypt, and remain there until I tell you; for Herod intends to search for the Child in order to destroy Him." So Joseph got up and took the Child and His mother while it was still night, and left for Egypt' (AMP). Although Jesus and His family survived, they did so as 'refugees', forfeiting any business Joseph may have had in Bethlehem, and undoubtedly travelling light. What a Saviour He is!

Isn't it amazing to think that Jesus Christ, the Prince of Glory, the One who left the splendour of heaven, would come to this earth to save humankind and, while here, didn't even have a roof over His own head? In other words, in His role as the Son of Man, Jesus identifies fully with the human plight of the homeless, the refugees, and with the poor, rejected and the suffering of this world.

Homelessness is an issue today which must be taken seriously. The Homeless Monitor report, which is carried out by researchers at Heriot Watt University and is a five-year study between 2011 and 2015, suggests that since the 2007 economic crisis and housing market downturn, rough sleeping in England has increased considerably and homelessness continues to rise at a frightening rate. Aside from England, many other parts of the UK and Ireland are affected by homelessness due to the economic situation and, additionally, because of the arrival of thousands of immigrants in the UK, most of whom have nowhere to live.

In this harsh age of austerity, one would assume people would have a greater sense of compassion for one another; on the contrary, however, the age of austerity has made the human race more selfish and ruthless, presumably in a bid to survive.

Many people haven't been able to cope with the rejection which followed the fallout from the recession. They see themselves as having been 'left to die' and, void of hope, they have even attempted suicide.

The world recession has led to the condemnation of many hard-working and sincere people, especially foreign immigrants who gain much less sympathy than previously. People in general are being offered less work, while zero-hours contracts are now common as multitudes find themselves in a precarious and disadvantaged position. Notably, poverty is no longer something that happens to the unemployed. It is also something that is happening to those moving in and out of low-paid jobs, and even those in full-time employment. The world has changed! This is the new world in which we live.

The biggest dilemma which is facing governments today and the question being asked is: Do we ignore these people, or do we try to help them? Do we leave them to die, or do we try to rescue and provide for them?

In the book of Genesis, after Cain had murdered his brother, Abel, he was asked by God where his brother was. Even though God already knew what had taken place, Cain replied, 'I do not know. Am I my brother's keeper?' (Genesis 4:9, NKJV)

The answer to Cain's cunning response was, yes! Cain was responsible for the welfare of his brother, but out of jealousy he chose to kill him instead. While no one can protect everyone, of course, every man remains his brother's keeper. We are not to commit violent acts against them or allow others to do so if we can prevent it. This obvious duty of care God rightfully demands of everyone, on the grounds of justice and love. Cain's reply and, indeed, the actions of Abraham and Sarah, indicate a total lack of compassion for a fellow human being.

Twice in the life of Joseph he was left to die by the people closest to him, and by people who were religious. Once, when he was betrayed by his brothers in Canaan, and later when he was let down by his master, Potiphar, who after he'd been wrongly accused of inappropriate behaviour with Potiphar's wife, chose to remove him from his house and place him in jail where he spent many years.

I wonder, did Potiphar discern that Joseph was innocent?

Even if he did, he didn't for a moment consider the pain he was about to inflict upon Joseph.

In many ways Abraham and Sarah did the exact same thing with Hagar and Ishmael. They had Isaac now. The people of Canaan were watching. If Ishmael wasn't the son of promise, then let him be sacrificed and leave the rest with God. This harsh attitude exists today, but it is not the love of a compassionate God.

While God may well have permitted the expulsion of Hagar and her son from the home of Abraham and Sarah, He still loved and cared for them and was interested in their welfare thereafter. Even if no one else empathised with them in their wilderness experience, God would always be there for them. What does this tell us? When the world is preoccupied, God sees the hopeless, homeless man and woman in their pain and sorrow. He cares, and even when the church walks by on the other side of the road, He can find someone else to help bind up their wounds – even a big-hearted radio presenter who doesn't profess to be a Christian!

I conclude this chapter with an extraordinary story I read about a pastor who brilliantly transformed himself into a homeless person and went to the 10,000-member church where he was to be introduced as the head pastor that same morning. As he paraded around his soon-to-be church for thirty minutes, while it was filling with people for the service, only three people out of the 10,000-strong gathering said hello to him.

He asked people for change to buy food – but was ignored. He went into the worship centre to sit down at the front of the church, only to be moved to the back by the ushers. He greeted people with a smile but was met with harsh stares, dirty looks, and people condescendingly glancing towards him. As he sat in the back of the church, he listened to the church announcements and such. When this had concluded, the elders went up to the platform and were excited to introduce the new pastor of the church to the congregation. 'Ladies and gentlemen, allow us to introduce to you our new pastor.'

The congregation looked around, clapping and naturally filled with joy and expectation. Then the homeless man sitting in the back stood up and proceeded towards the front of the church. The clapping ceased and all eyes were now on the man whom many had rejected earlier. He walked up to the altar and took the microphone from the elders (some of whom knew what was happening) and paused for a moment; then he recited some of the most powerful and convicting words in the New Testament – a passage of Scripture which has convicted many Christians throughout the centuries:

> Then the King will say to those on his right, 'Come, you who are blessed by my Father; take your inheritance, the kingdom prepared for you since the creation of the world. For I was hungry and you gave me something to eat, I was thirsty and you gave me something to drink, I was a stranger and you invited me in, I needed clothes and you clothed me, I was sick and you looked after me, I was in prison and you came to visit me.' Then the righteous will answer him, 'Lord, when did we see you hungry and feed you, or thirsty and give you something to drink? When did we see you a stranger and invite you in, or needing clothes and clothe you? When did we see you sick or in prison and go to visit you?' The King will reply, 'Truly I tell you, whatever you did for one of the least of these brothers and sisters of mine, you did for me.' (Matthew 25:34–40, NIV 2011)

After the pastor had recited this, he made the following remarks:

'Today I see a gathering of people, not a church of Jesus Christ. The world has enough people, but not enough disciples. When will you decide to become disciples?' He then dismissed the service until the next week, leaving many of his new flock to consider their ways. Here was a challenge to a congregation to not only begin to consider loving the hungry, homeless and the sick in a much deeper and compassionate way, but also to start loving the unloved.[2]

Walking in the footsteps of Jesus Christ is quite a responsibility. It should be more than just talk. It ought to be a lifestyle where others can see the love of God shining through. Let's not pass the homeless, the poor and the needy and those less fortunate. When we have 'opportunity' as Paul puts it, let us 'do good … and especially to those who are of the household of faith' (Galatians 6:10, ESV).

For further thought, prayer and reflection

- How much does the issue of homelessness register with you? Is this growing epidemic the concern of someone else, or is God calling you personally to assist someone who has no home?
- Did you ever consider the fact that Jesus said he had nowhere to lay His head? Do you believe this makes Him more able to deal with the pain of homeless people?
- How can your walk with God be improved by caring for your homeless brother, sister or friend?
- What great quality is required – according to the parable of the Good Samaritan?

Notes
1. turnbir.com.
2. Story paraphrased. See snopes.com.

Seventeen:
Loving our Neighbour?

Your own safety is at stake when your neighbour's wall is ablaze.
(Horace)[1]

The name Hagar (which we know means 'stranger') is revered in the Islamic faith and recognised in all Abrahamic faiths. Her son, Ishmael, is also a man from whom all Muslims and many Arabs still believe they have descended.

When Sarah and Abraham cast Hagar out of their house, this decision was not just racial intolerance, but spiritual elitism was also evident. Remember what Sarah said to Abraham: 'Drive out this maid and her son, for the son of this maid shall not be an heir with my son Isaac' (Genesis 21:10, NASB), or as the New Living Translation of this verse reads: 'So she turned to Abraham and demanded, "Get rid of that slave woman and her son. He is not going to share the inheritance with my son, Isaac. I won't have it!"'

There is more than a hint of spiritual elitism in this very

statement – something we are all-too familiar with today. Why, for example, is there so much trouble in the world? Is it not due to a similar lust for power, territory and personal glory which produces religious fanaticism and deep spiritual pride?

Spiritual elitism is the assumption that salvation is only for certain persons or members of certain classes or groups by virtue of their perceived superiority, as in intellect, social status, or financial resources.

This is contrary to the teaching of the words of John 3:16 which remind us how God so loved 'the world' and sent His only son to die so that whosoever called upon him would be saved and favoured of God. God's intention is for everybody to be saved, delivered, healed, protected, and preserved. We all have access to God's grace and mercy, the same birthright, the same God, and the same love from the Father.

The religions of Judaism, Christianity and Islam have been at each other's throats for centuries and, if anything, the historic tension between the three Abrahamic faiths is escalating. Why? Because they all believe they are entitled to Abraham's promise.

Jews and Christians look to Isaac as the promised son, and maintain a 'we are the people' stance, while followers of Islam believe Ishmael was the promised one and declare 'we are right and you are wrong'. Some extreme Islamic fundamentalists believe this now gives them the right to aggressively pursue this promise, even to the extent where murder and great suffering is acceptable which, of course, it isn't and never will be.

Much of the war in our world today is provoked by religious fanaticism and by people needing to belong to something; people with tribal instincts, not God instincts. Tribalism keeps strife at the forefront of a nation and announces 'my God is stronger than yours'. Tribalism is for people who believe they are right and the other side is wrong. Sadly, tribalism has today not only infiltrated the Christian church, it appears to have managed to poison many people's hearts within numerous other religions. This has caused widespread trouble, suffering and death in extraordinary proportions. Even politicians and public figures get embroiled in disputes which reveal their own deep-rooted tribalism. Platitudes do not make for a lasting peace anywhere. On the contrary, they stoke the fires of hatred and an uneasy division between already fractured religious groups.

This is most grievous in the sight of God. God's love is a global love and is totally impartial. God's ideal is unity, not separation. God's kingdom will not only include the multicultural, but the multicoloured. John wrote in the book of Revelation: 'After this I beheld, and lo, a great multitude, which no man could number, of all nations, and kindreds, and people, and tongues, stood before the throne, and before the Lamb, clothed with white robes, and palms in their hands' (Revelation 7:9).

In his book entitled *Racism and the Church*, James E. Collins writes: 'The gospel of Christ knows no colour, gender, denomination, social class or any other separation. It crosses all barriers – to set all people free.'[2]

Genealogical rivalry between religions such as Christianity, Islam and Judaism threatens the entire safety and stability of the earth. Rabbi Jonathan Sacks writes in his book *Not in God's Name*:

Too often in the history of religion, people have killed in the name of the God of life, waged war in the name of the God of peace, hated in the name of the God of love and practiced cruelty in the name of the God of compassion. When this happens, God speaks, sometimes in a still, small voice almost inaudible beneath the clamour of those claiming to speak on his behalf. What he says at such times is: Not in my name.[3]

Rabbi Jonathan Sacks adds: 'When religion becomes a zero-sum conceit – i.e., my religion is the only "right" path to God, therefore your religion is by definition "wrong" – violence between peoples of different beliefs is the only natural outcome.'[4]

The increase in violence by Islamic extremists presents the twenty-first century with a very interesting consideration at a crucial time in history. How do we respond to Islamic extremists and religious violence? Do we respond with similar violence, or do nothing and risk being wiped out altogether? It's a complex and difficult dilemma.

Can we learn to be peacemakers and forgive, both at a personal and national level? This is the all-important question being asked of the citizens of our current generation. It's a question we will consider in more detail later. War has been tried and war has failed. Paul wrote 'If it be possible, as much as lieth in you, live peaceably with all men' (Romans 12:18).

Peace, of course, is not always possible, and for a variety of reasons. No matter how hard we try, some people do not want to live in peace with their neighbour, but the point is obvious. We must become peacemakers if we are to please God and if we are to see an end to violence and counter-violence.

Because a solution cannot currently be found to the world's discord, a good place to start, in terms of calming the storm, would be if the church could begin by 'loving its neighbour', regardless of religious or cultural differences. In our multicultural society, loving our neighbour and extending kindness and hospitality to those of other faiths is not only imperative; I believe it is the very heart of God. True, nations must defend their people and be vigilant not to accommodate terrorists with sinister motives, but far too often this approach is used an excuse for not loving their neighbours. From the book of Genesis to Revelation, God has never changed His mind in relation to how we are to love and care for one another, irrespective of religious or ethnic tradition. This view is well documented within both the Old and New Testaments.

For example, God commanded the second generation of Israelites in the Old Testament to bless and love their neighbours, to live side by side with them, even to treat the stranger in their midst with respect. The Bible not only commands Christians to welcome and love the stranger at their gate, it declares: 'Thou shalt neither vex a stranger, nor oppress him: for ye were strangers in the land of Egypt' (Exodus 22:21).

Moses encouraged the children of Israel not to oppress or criticise their neighbours, but to bring to mind the hardship they themselves went through when they were in Egypt.

In the Old Testament it's clear that the Bible encourages cultures and individuals to encompass care beyond their own borders. How is this same principle revealed in the New Testament? When a lawyer asked Jesus what he needed to do in order to inherit eternal life, Jesus replied: '… love the Lord thy God with all thy heart, and with all thy soul, and with all thy strength, and with all thy mind; and thy neighbour as thyself' (Luke 10:27).

It's amazing how many God-fearing and conscientious Christians are quite happy to try to fulfil the first commandment of Christ which is to love God with all of our hearts… yet the same group doesn't always appear to be equally concerned with the second commandment which is effectively the loving of others.

Who is our neighbour? Our neighbour is not just the person living next door to us; our neighbour is everyone we meet, and the stranger who originates from every religious and ethnic experience. Our neighbour is the homeless man, the Muslim, the Jewish person, the black and the white person, the gay man, the transgendered person, the atheist, the racist, the drug addict and the alcoholic.

God's Word encourages the Christian to reach out to people of all descriptions and religions with greater love, understanding, compassion and humility. Of course, loving one's neighbour doesn't mean we always agree with them or their lifestyles, but treating our neighbour with respect is God's ideal for the sincere Christian.

What am I saying? It's possible to love our neighbour but still keep up our fence!

Abraham is known to be revered today by approximately 2.5 billion Christians, 1.6 billion Muslims and by 13 million Jews. The obvious question is, why? Why or how did he have such a huge impact upon so many cultures and religions? The answer may well be because he prayed for people of all cultures, and his prayers extended far beyond his own kindred. He prayed for King Abimelech and his family, for Sodom, and his constant prayers on behalf of others of all backgrounds proved Abraham had a heart for the lost. Such was Abraham's obligation to respect people from every upbringing, there's even a strong suggestion within Judaism that he would not bless any of Ishmael's wives until he was sure they were given to hospitality of strangers.

What am I saying? People of different religions to Christianity are not second-class citizens and should not be treated as such. They are souls whom God loves and desires to save just as much as those who have been converted. God's command is that we love one another regardless of any spiritual differences.

With the dramatic increase of Islamic violence in various countries today, many Christians are finding great difficulty in both forgiving and loving their Muslim neighbour. This is quite understandable, given some of the awful atrocities which have taken place. But God wants us to forgive and love not just our neighbour, but the stranger in our midst – and yes, even our enemies. Today many Christians fear their enemies. God says, 'Love your enemies.'

In the wake of the slaughter of around 150 students in Kenya in 2015, the Archbishop of Canterbury, Justin Welby, called on Christians to use nonviolent means of resistance when faced with persecution by extremists, stating it would lead to better relations. What a test of Christian love and tolerance this will prove!

Opening a school for Syrian refugees in 2015, the youngest-ever winner of the Nobel Peace Prize, a young Muslim girl, Malala Yousafzai, urged political representatives to invest in 'books' not 'bullets' to help promote peace and change the atmosphere of a volatile world. She was saying, wars are won by weapons, but it takes ideas to win peace.

Here we have both Christian and Muslim visionaries doing their bit to help heal broken relationships between people of different religions.

Malala believes that education, theology and debate, not violence and counter-violence is what's required to help calm the religious storm in our world, while Justin Welby is exhorting a loving and gracious response to religious provocation.

In the future, the power of words and the strength of arguments will win the day. Right theology – loving our neighbour as ourselves – is the fastest road to peace for all nations.

This almost sounds too easy, yet loving one's neighbour is the Bible's answer to racial intolerance and religious bigotry and to the actions of people who have caused great hurt to their fellow human beings. Small things become great when done with love. Joel Osteen says 'Being right is overrated. Jesus said "Blessed are the peacemakers." He didn't say blessed are those who are right.' Many broken relationships can be healed when love, kindness and understanding is present, especially between opposing religions.

God is simply asking us to be more loving, compassionate and understanding of our neighbour. The unity of God asks us to respect the stranger, the outsider, the alien, because even though they are not in our image – their ethnicity, faith or culture are not ours – nonetheless, they are in God's image and God is universal. Billy Graham wrote:

The devil did not create the various races. Instead, God created them and gave them their unique identity. The Bible says, 'From one man (Adam) he made every nation of men, that they should inhabit the whole earth; and he determined the times set for them and the exact places where they should live' (Acts 17:26).

But God did not create the strife between races, nor did He intend for it to be that way. Strife between races and ethnic groups comes from sin – and sin resides in the human heart. The Bible says, 'What causes fights and quarrels among you? Don't they come from your desires that battle within you?' (James 4:1). When one group or one race claims it is superior to another, pride has taken control – and pride is a sin.

Instead, God wants us to learn to accept each other and love each other – and this becomes possible, as we turn our lives over to Christ and allow him to change us from within. When we allow sin to rule us, we easily give in to hate and anger. But Christ's Spirit gives us hope, even for those we once despised. The Bible says, 'But the fruit of the Spirit is love' (Galatians 5:22).

It has often been said that the ground at the foot of the cross is level – and it is true. No matter who we are, we need Christ's forgiveness and grace. Have you come to Him for the forgiveness and new life He offers?[5]

In our multicultural society, loving our neighbour and extending kindness and hospitality to those of other faiths is not only imperative; I believe it is the very heart of God.

Hagar's account reminds us how the gospel of Jesus Christ transcends all religious barriers and is for everyone who will receive it. God's command to every believer is to reach out to people of all faiths with the good news of the gospel. This is evident by one of Christ's last commands to His followers: 'Go therefore and make disciples of all nations, baptizing them in the name of the Father and of the Son and of the Holy Spirit' (Matthew 28:19, ESV).

While spiritually elite people have convinced themselves that the gospel is only for them or certain groups, the truly great communicators of the gospel understand that all people are 'dead in trespasses and sins' (Ephesians 2:1, NKJV), whether they are nominal Christians, Muslim, atheist or pagan, or from any other standpoint. The Bible makes it perfectly clear that we are all sinners in need of the Saviour. It is vital today not to hinder those who have a heart to reach people of different ethnic backgrounds with the gospel of peace because of animosity or prejudice towards people of other faiths. This is because there are many Christians doing great work in an attempt to reach our wider secular cultures and challenging their traditions and beliefs.

When these same cultures are criticised, it conceals God's love for them and discourages them from being converted. It can also place the lives of both Christians and non-Christians in danger.

Those who truly love Jesus and are serious about sharing His message with the world will love as Jesus loved and love their neighbour, regardless of skin colour or background.

The mission of a Christian hasn't changed. Christ's message of love to a broken world has still to be shared with every nation, tribe and people. Christianity promotes a gospel of peace, love and reconciliation, not war, hatred, superiority and revenge.

For further thought, prayer and reflection

- Why do you believe there is so much trouble in the world today?
- Is there a better alternative to solving this trouble than with further violence?
- Is spiritual elitism a problem for you or your church?
- Why is racism and spiritual elitism wrong in general and within the church?
- Are you a natural peacemaker, or do you enjoy a good argument?
- Is arguing and fighting from God – or is peace the way of God?
- After the commandment to love God, what are we required to do?
- Are you prepared to be more understanding to people of other religions in order to win them to God?
- What does the gospel of Christ and Christianity promote?

Notes

1. brainyquote.com.
2. James E. Collins, *Racism and the Church* (Revere, MA: Eagle Heights, 2013).
3. Rabbi Jonathan Sacks, *Not in God's Name* (London: Hodder & Stoughton, 2015), p. 3.
4. Sacks, *Not in God's Name*.
5. http://billygraham.org/answer/where-did-all-the-different-races-come-from.

Eighteen:
No Man Cared for Her Soul

No one knows for certain the impact they have on the lives of other people. Oftentimes, we have no clue. Yet we push it just the same.
(Jay Asher)[1]

As Hagar trooped into the wilderness of Beersheba with Ishmael, leaving a home she'd been part of for almost a quarter of a century, the fear, hurt and confusion she experienced must have been overwhelming.

As she negotiated her way through the unpredictable landscape of that same wilderness, knowing there was no way back to Abraham and Sarah's home, her sandals burning in the hot sun and her throat choking on dust, she would have felt so intensely abandoned and helpless.

Let's not forget, this is not just a story. It's a true-life event.

With just a bottle of water and a loaf of bread to keep her and Ishmael alive, every step Hagar took would have been a painful step – yet the Bible records that no one came to her rescue. Unless God miraculously intervened, she was literally walking to her grave. Her faith shattered for only doing what she believed was right; she not only felt rejected by God's people, but also by God Himself.

While she probably didn't expect Abraham and Sarah to tolerate the intimidation of Ishmael towards Isaac, their new son, neither would she have envisaged being cast out into the harshness of the Arabian desert and left to die. That act of love she had performed for Abraham and Sarah all those years ago when she gave birth to Ishmael didn't seem to matter now. In Hagar's case it was a case of personal survival, sink or swim.

This second exile would teach Hagar a powerful lesson; there are few friends in a wilderness, and all that is left are painful memories from a life that's past.

In his book entitled **Thirteen Reasons Why,** *Jay Asher wrote:* *'No one knows for certain the impact they have on the lives of other people. Oftentimes, we have no clue. Yet we push it just the same.'²*

When Abraham and Sarah condemned Hagar and her son to the ferocity of a Middle Eastern desert, they surely couldn't have been conscious of the pain and suffering they were inflicting on them – or just how much it would hurt and influence their lives. They had inflicted wounds which would take many months, if not years, to heal.

Anne Graham Lotz wrote in *Wounded by God's People*: 'Wounds from a "Christian sword" heal slowly because they seem to hurt the most and penetrate the deepest.'³ In Hagar's case we will never know how long it took for her own wounds to heal, but certainly they wouldn't have disappeared overnight. These were deep, personal wounds which were caused by people she'd loved and assumed loved her.

The wilderness has been described as an uncivilised, unpopulated and unwelcoming place. In a spiritual sense, of course, it's a place where God prevents us from taking care of ourselves and positions us where we have to rely solely on Him instead. While most people fear the wilderness, even supposing it might destroy them, the truth is the result of a wilderness experience not only builds character; it can also lead to a closer walk with God. Nancy Wynne Newhall wrote, 'The wilderness holds answers to more questions than we have yet learned to ask.'[4]

Out of any God-ordained wilderness emerge consecration and cleansing, change, teaching and spiritual recovery and renewal – and yes, sometimes even forgiveness and reconciliation. During wilderness experiences, the Holy Spirit transforms us from the inside out and helps us confront all of the hurt and offence from our past.

Our profession, social groups, church life, our relationships, marriage, home, our finances and even our understanding all come under the spotlight as God prepares us for a new life. There is much to be learned in the backwoods about God, people and ourselves; nevertheless, getting delivered from such remoteness can't come quick enough for most of us.

Hagar and Ishmael had lost everything. The worst part, however, was the fact that they were no longer in control of their lives. They would have soon noticed an absence of divine assistance and spiritual grace, something that was always evident while they were in Canaan and other places with Abraham. The strength they once exhibited no longer seemed to be there. Wounds that Hagar had kept buried for years also began to resurface, while the lack of financial assistance brought some dire new challenges for Hagar and her young son. With no income or provision, Hagar had no way to provide, not only for her, but also for the needs of Ishmael.

Abraham had always provided everything for Hagar, but now Hagar simply had to make it on her own. It was like a recession visited her and Ishmael personally, and she must have wondered what on earth was going on, and what she had done to deserve this. Have you noticed when financial hardship arrives in our lives, it's usually followed by doubt?

Had Hagar been wrong to let Abraham and Sarah talk her into giving birth to their child? Had she been wrong not to intervene more when Ishmael was mocking Isaac? Was she to blame for lording it over Sarah about Ishmael when Sarah was barren? Had she grieved Almighty God in some way that would provoke Him to remove His blessing from her life? Those were natural questions – questions we might have asked ourselves if things had imploded in a similar way. When things turn sour, we often examine our lives to see what we might have done wrong. Yet many times, wilderness experiences are not caused by something we've done wrong, but are just a part of life.

I believe there are people all over the world today asking a similar question to Hagar's, having found themselves in the midst of a testing trial. They once had everything – a good job, a nice car, social events galore and two or three holidays per year; they had position, prestige and plenty of money; then the global recession hit or an incident occurred that left them almost destitute and using food banks for the first time, or having to borrow money regularly from family and friends just to get by. Suddenly they wonder what caused their demise. They ask questions such as: 'Why is this happening to me?' or 'Does God not see me in my need and in my situation?' 'Where is God?' they scream.

How we respond during a wilderness period can determine if we survive and make it back again. Do we have a positive or negative approach to our unexpected sojourn in the wilderness?

For example, from Sinai, God led the Israelites through the great and terrible wilderness to Kadesh (the border of the Promised Land). Moses sent twelve spies, one from each of the twelve tribes of Israel, into Canaan to explore the land. The spies returned with glowing reports of the fruitfulness of the land. They brought back samples of figs and pomegranates and a cluster of grapes so large it had to be carried between two men on a pole. The majority of the spies, however, voted against the invasion of the land because of the huge inhabitants of Canaan and fortified cities 'walled up to heaven' (Deuteronomy 1:28). It was a report of doom. Yet two of the spies, Joshua and Caleb, brought back a report full of faith and encouragement. They were trusting God despite the obstacles ahead!

Similarly, during our own desperate times, when obstacles and famine seem insurmountable, we learn to live by every word that proceeds from the mouth of God for every part of our lives. In short: We learn to look up and trust in God!

When we reach a stage where our previous means of support completely dries up, we have no alternative but to trust in God and Him alone.

Financial experts believe that many people today are less than three missed mortgage payments away from bankruptcy following the world recessions. Lack, famine and even drought has plummeted many parts of the world into financial chaos.

You don't have to be a single mother such as Hagar to experience this wilderness. Many people today are struggling in life and it seems the world is caving in around them. They search for answers and pray for deliverance but still find themselves in the same position. What's beautiful about Hagar's story, however, is the personal care God displays towards Hagar and her son. When all seemed lost, God saw her in her need and pain. This gives us hope that God can meet us in our own times of drought. For the second time in her short life, an angel of the Lord came searching after her and found her by a spring of water in the desert. So, clearly, the Lord was observing events in her life day by day and guiding her. Think about it! The One who came to seek that which was lost had found Hagar in all her distress. Here we see the Good Shepherd's care for the wandering sheep. Sheep are stubborn, but the Good Shepherd loves and cares for them. Though Abraham showed no concern for Hagar, God cared for this defenceless woman. His love extended to people of all backgrounds and considered the entire family of Abraham as numerous as the sands on the seashore.

While Abraham and Sarah had no qualms in writing Hagar and Ishmael off, God's heart could not forget even a poor, single Egyptian mother wandering in the desert. Who am I talking to out there? It doesn't matter where you live or what you're currently going through, God loves you and sees you in your pain. Have you been experiencing a brutal wilderness, a place that has left you feeling isolated and even incapacitated? God says, 'I will make a way through the wilderness in your life.'

Hagar's second spell in the wilderness was no accident. God was about to birth a nation through Ishmael. When God is announcing something He often uses a wilderness to do it. The world would use the city and the most populated area, but God uses the desert and the most barren place. The Bible tells us that John the Baptist was 'the voice of one crying in the wilderness'

(John 1:23), a phrase used in the Gospels to refer to John the Baptist in the prime of his preaching and as he announced the first coming of Jesus. This verse is also quoted from the book of Isaiah, written 700 hundred years previously, which reads: 'The voice of one crying in the wilderness: 'Prepare the way of the LORD; Make straight in the desert A highway for our God' (Isaiah 40:3, NKJV).

God used a desert prophet, not a Jerusalem Jesuit to announce the arrival of the Son of God to the world. God often uses the weak things of the world to confound the wise.

It's interesting how Hagar isn't passed over in the book of Genesis as some may try to suggest; moreover, Hagar mattered to the Almighty as much as anyone else.

In other words, even when God's creation fails to live up to His covenant requirements, God remains a caring and a faithful God. Can you picture just how compassionate the love of God is? Despite the fact that Abraham had been unfaithful in his dealings with Hagar, God remained totally faithful to her. No one cared for her soul, but God cared, and ultimately this would prove to be enough.

Psalm 142 contains a prayer of David when he was forced to live in a cave. David, while hiding from King Saul, had been deserted by all his friends. He was in the wilderness of rejection and poverty and in many ways his life was a representation of the rejection Hagar endured. In one of the saddest verses in the Bible, David commented: 'Look on my right hand and see, For there is no one who acknowledges me; Refuge has failed me; No one cares for my soul' (Psalm 142:4, NKJV). Hagar would have identified so well with the words of Psalm 142 and verse 4 – 'I looked on my right hand, and beheld, but there was no man that would know me' (KJV).

This was Hagar. No friends, no helpers, and none to stand with her or undertake her defence. Hagar couldn't even find a friendly smile in the wilderness. She was totally estranged from everyone and everything. If the same technology we have today had been available in Hagar's time, then her phone would not have rung, her emails would not have been replied to, her job applications would have been ignored, her former friends would have turned cold and indifferent, keeping her at a constant distance. Hagar would have been merely tolerated, but certainly not celebrated!

Once popular and prosperous by comparison, suddenly no one wanted to know her. Whether she lived or died was no concern of anyone. She had been thrown out as an outcast. She was dwelling in no man's land, in brutal deserts where no one cared to have her and no one cared about her.

What a dark place this is to be! Her enemies must have been delighted to learn that the once-prominent Hagar who was previously secure in Abraham's abode was now without a home of her own and without a friend in the world. Her secret jealous rivals would have been literally rubbing their hands with glee at such a development. How broken she must have felt, being deserted in this way by people she assumed loved her. Trudging through the sand, she had no shelter from the sun, and no water, and seemingly no God. Ishmael, too, must have been cursing his father with every step and bemoaning his general lot in life.

Both would be forced into the same corner as David found himself in. Buried in a cave, complaining about how he had no refuge and life was so unfair, suddenly, instead of crying within, David began to cry out in prayer.

This was the place where God was leading Hagar and Ishmael also – the place of prayer and supplication – the place of crying out to God from the depths of their hearts – a place where deep would begin to call unto deep and supernatural answers to prayer were miraculously about to follow. God was challenging Hagar to recall the prayers of the mighty Abraham which had seen him delivered from many situations over the years.

Hagar may have found herself in the middle of nowhere, but in the middle of nowhere she was just about to find herself.

For further thought, prayer and reflection

- Do you consider carefully the impact your decisions might have upon other people before you make them?
- Have you been deeply wounded by someone close to you, and has this caused great pain in your life?
- Have these wounds healed, or are you still struggling with this issue in your life?
- Have you ever had a wilderness experience which has isolated you from your friends, family and normal areas of daily life?
- Do you question yourself or God when you are in a wilderness?
- Are you a recovering victim of the global recession, and what have you learned about life during this period of economic downfall?

Notes

1. Jay Asher, *Thirteen Reasons Why* (London: Penguin, 2009).
2. Asher, *Thirteen Reasons Why*.
3. Anne Graham Lotz, *Wounded by God's People* (London: Hodder & Stoughton, 2013).
4. goodreads.com.

Nineteen:
Stop Crying – and Start Crying Out

*Crying is the only way your eyes speak when your mouth can't
explain how things made your heart broken.*
(C.L. Gillmore)[1]

One of the dangers I have discovered about life in the wilderness
is the tendency to begin to look inwardly. The longer we travel
that hot, dusty, parched road, the more egocentric and self-
interested we can become. Instead of living a victorious life, we
begin to see ourselves as nothing more than victims. 'Woe is me!'
is a frequent daily thought. Like Elijah, who just wanted to die
under a juniper tree because he felt that he was no better than his
fathers, we all possess the tendency to hold a similar pity-party
and almost give up on everyone, including ourselves.

This is a hazardous place to be. It's a place where we can
become extremely vulnerable, especially to the devices of Satan,
who continually plants seeds of doubt in our heads and even
tempts us to turn away from trusting in God. It was while Jesus

was in the wilderness, directly after He'd been declared the Son of God and the Saviour of the world, that the devil tempted Him with great privileges and special tokens of divine favour.

The Bible says: 'Again, the devil taketh him up into an exceeding high mountain, and sheweth him all the kingdoms of the world, and the glory of them; And saith unto him, All these things will I give thee, if thou wilt fall down and worship me. Then saith Jesus unto him, Get thee hence, Satan: for it is written, Thou shalt worship the Lord thy God, and him only shalt thou serve' (Matthew 4:8–10).

When we present our woes to ourselves it can overwhelm us, and that's when Satan comes, but when we present our burdens to the Lord, we lighten our load and bring some perspective back into the situation. Peter wrote: 'Casting all your care upon him; for he careth for you' (1 Peter 5:7).

As we explored earlier, God doesn't always answer our prayers according to our timing, but one thing is certain: God is a prayer-hearing and a prayer-answering God. Whether we are on the mountain-top or in the valley, He wants us to freely bring our concerns and requests to Him first. Paul wrote: 'Be careful [anxious] for nothing; but in every thing by prayer and supplication with thanksgiving let your requests be made known unto God' (Philippians 4:6).

Abraham was a great man of prayer. He knew how and when to approach God. True, as we've already seen, he was not a perfect man and he had many flaws, he could even be thoughtless and insensitive, but he was, nevertheless, a man who knew how to cry out to Almighty God. The fact that he left a trail of altars behind him everywhere he went proved how much Abraham believed in the power of prayer.

Over the years, he'd prayed for Hagar's son and for the wicked city of Sodom and he no doubt prayed for his wayward nephew Lot and for his family, community and nation. Come to think of it, Hagar would have witnessed some of this devotion to prayer by Abraham, and this would have left an indelible mark upon her life. Regardless of the fact that Hagar and Abraham didn't part on the best of terms, Abraham was a man she wouldn't easily forget, and not only for negative reasons. Abraham would have had an immense influence on Hagar in a positive sense, too.

It can be years before we realise the true reason why God put someone else in our lives. In fact, it's only later we understand just what this other person has imparted to us. In Hagar's case, it was an impartation to 'pray' or to 'cry out' unto the living God. There's no evidence that she cried out right away, of course, but when things became suitably bad it wouldn't be long before Hagar reflected on the past and recalled those constant pictures of her husband, Abraham, locked away in the secret place of prayer.

Initially Hagar was probably far too wounded to pray. She was shell-shocked by the actions of Abraham and Sarah and if, anything, prayer, worship and all things 'religious' would only have reminded her of her relationship with them. Prayer was the last thing she wanted to engage in. After all, 'What an old hypocrite Abraham was,' she must have thought to herself. 'Imagine praying to God and then treating people the way he treated me and Ishmael.' If Hagar did retain such thoughts, they would have held her back from her miracle because not only would there have been bitterness, but disappointment too.

We can speculate all day long regarding the reasons behind Hagar's initial reticence to pray and, yes, it may have been due to Abraham and Sarah's harsh treatment of both her and Ishmael when they were removed from their home; notwithstanding, she didn't appear to seek God in any visible way. The Bible says:

'When the water in the skin was gone, she put the boy under one of the bushes. Then she went off and sat down nearby, about a bow-shot away, for she thought, "I cannot watch the boy die." And as she sat there nearby, she began to sob' (Genesis 21:15,16, NIV 1984).

Two words leap from this text – the words 'die' and 'sob'. What a sorry picture this paints of just how cut off and broken poor Hagar was. Convinced both she and Ishmael would die in the wilderness, it was natural that tears of regret and sadness would result. Her world had collapsed and her dreams lay in tatters. What else could she do but weep and sob?

C.L. Gilmore wrote: 'Crying is the only way your eyes speak when your mouth can't explain how things made your heart broken.'[2]

Hagar therefore is a striking picture of us all. Often we can end up in a place feeling mentally, physically, emotionally, materially and spiritually ruined, and we wonder how we got there. The psalmist cried out: 'I shall not die, but live, and declare the works of the LORD' (Psalm 118:17). In other words he is saying 'don't quit', 'don't give up', 'live and testify to the goodness of God'.

If you've ever been in a wilderness you'll know that initially it's the fault of everyone else and not you. There are plenty of people to blame and Hagar had her own list of so-called perpetrators. For a start, there was Pharaoh for giving her away and evicting her from her homeland in the first place, then there was Abraham and Sarah for deserting and betraying her, there was Ishmael for his 'stupid mocking' of Isaac, there was the birth of Isaac which seemingly ruined everything for Hagar and Ishmael… oh, and there was God also. You will notice that nowhere in that list appears the name – Hagar.

Hagar was wronged, but not perfect herself. And neither was Ishmael. Sometimes our pride can isolate us due to a failure to call upon God. It's almost as though we would rather die than cry out to God – and this appeared to be Hagar. Whether it was pride or independence or rebellion that prevented her from crying out to God I don't know, but something in her flesh didn't like to admit that she didn't have everything under control. Something reacted when she became conscious of her need for someone else, someone greater and someone much more powerful than herself.

The world teaches us today that if there's no way, then we should find a way, but what happens when God blocks every way, even the way that we try to find? What happens when He closes every road and shuts down every avenue? What do we do then? No one is stronger than God. The Bible says in the book of Revelation: 'What he opens no one can shut, and what he shuts no one can open' (Revelation 3:7, NIV 2011).

Are you in a wilderness of confusion and getting no answers at present? Perhaps you're a Christian, a Muslim, a Mormon, a Jehovah's Witness or a non-religious person and you have been in a wilderness for some time. Maybe you have believed the lie that God has abandoned you and no longer loves you. Are you tired of trying to find God and wish with all your heart and soul that God would come and find you?

Then read the following amazing story of how God can reach and save you in your own wilderness if you will but cry out to Him.

Mosab Hassan Yousef was brought up in Ramallah, in the Palestinian West Bank in 1978. He was raised as a Muslim and was a staunch follower of Islam. His father, Sheikh Hassan Yousef, is well known as a founding leader of Hamas, internationally recognized as a terrorist organization and a group responsible for numerous suicide bombings and other lethal attacks against Israel.

Mosab quickly joined the organisation and was often imprisoned by the Shin Bet, the Israeli intelligence service. But during one of those prison stints he soon realised that Hamas was torturing its own people in a determined search for traitors. It was at this point that Mosab started to wonder who his enemies really were – Israel? Hamas? America?

Locked up in an Israeli cell, Mosab received the opportunity to work as a spy for the Shin Bet.

He accepted this opening, but initially with the intention of betraying the Israelis which he assumed would help protect his father and family. Something dramatic was to follow, however. Convicted by the Holy Spirit, he suddenly began to understand the hypocrisy within Hamas; but he also had his heart and eyes opened to the truth of the gospel and, for the first time in his life, became aware that Christianity was the only way to God and true salvation. In his powerfully written book, *Son of Hamas*[3], he tells the story of how a simple invitation to a gospel meeting handed to him at the Damascus Gate in Jerusalem helped change his life. He nearly didn't attend the meeting, but decided he had nothing to lose by going.

He accepted the invitation and was so impressed with what he heard he decided to obtain a copy of the New Testament. When Mosab got alone with God he began to read Matthew chapter five and the discourse by the Lord Jesus Christ on forgiveness, peace and loving one's enemies, his heart melted and he became a Christian right there and then. He cried unto the living God and asked for mercy and repented of all his sins of the past during his days as a terrorist.

Mosab learned about Christianity being a religion of peace, love and forgiveness and when God opened his eyes to the words of Christ, he saw the religion of Christianity in a different light. From that point on, Mosab used his position to save lives on both sides of the conflict. Remarkably he worked as a double agent within Hamas for nearly ten years without being suspected and became a vital intelligence asset for the Israeli government while he served side-by-side with his father within the upper ranks of Hamas. Naturally this eventually led to his life being threatened and he has since sought political asylum in America. His story is a truly extraordinary tale of just how God can reach people of every religion - even the most hostile of people with the power of the gospel.

What's keeping you from crying out to God? The same angel that was watching over Mosab Yousef was also watching over Hagar and this same angel is watching over you.

God loved the people back in Canaan, He certainly loved Abraham and Sarah, but God's love would find Hagar, too. He was very conscious of her situation, of her tears and her fears. She was at her wits' end and the fact is, she had nothing left in her material cupboard and even less in her spiritual tank. Can you picture Hagar lying on the ground with Ishmael just in front of her? She was probably on her knees, swaying, wailing from within her soul. This is the picture of how God responds to people who eventually cry out for help.

This raises another interesting question: Do we believe God is waiting to hear our cry and respond to it? I'm not speaking of begging God, but praying with sincerity and a power that touches heaven's throne. I'm talking about crying out from the depths of your heart. The Bible says: 'The effectual fervent prayer of a righteous man availeth much' (James 5:16). Joseph Prince wrote: 'Just a groan will reach God's throne.'[4]

In the Old Testament, the psalmist wrote: 'In my distress I called upon the LORD, and cried unto my God: he heard my voice out of his temple, and my cry came before him, even into his ears' (Psalm 18:6).

Hagar was surrounded by hell. The snares of death confronted both her and her son. This was not the time to be silent. She desperately needed to call upon the Lord and cry to Him for help, not suffer on in her hurt, bitterness and disappointment. Abraham, Sarah and those back in Canaan were getting on with their lives; meanwhile, Hagar and Ishmael were facing certain death unless something dramatic took place.

Over the years, Hagar had observed Abraham cry out to God and fight many battles of his own in the same way Jesus did in that closet of sincere prayer. She had no doubt watched the Almighty lovingly and tenderly answer many of Abraham's prayers regarding his business and family and future generations. Now it was her turn!

Could she possibly do the same thing? Would God respond to her prayers in the same way? If ever there was a time to find out, this was it. Indeed, was this the moment when Hagar asked Abraham's God to become her God? Did she have her own salvation experience after all she'd been through? This may be conjecture, but many others have come to God in difficult circumstances and we cannot always assume what has or hasn't taken place in the heart of an individual in relation to spiritual matters. Surely it would be inconceivable to believe that someone who was twice visited by an angel and delivered from death and destruction by the Almighty could resist such a loving, caring and compassionate God.

Perhaps for years your pastor has being praying you through difficult times, or others have been bearing you up on eagle's wings when you've faced major dilemmas. Yet all of a sudden your situation is so grave it demands that you personally call out to this same caring and compassionate God. Don't wait another moment to do it. Don't wait until the house burns down to pray; pray so that the fire doesn't start in the first place.

Hagar's life had imploded. Her son was poised to die under a bush and, with no water or food left, she would inevitably be next. It no longer mattered who was to blame for their demise, or how they got to the point of death; the only thing that mattered was the survival of both Ishmael and herself. What had she got to lose by crying unto God?

It was now or never!

Pray or die!

Plead or bleed!

Call or fall!

Time to stop crying, and start 'crying out' and see what the God of heaven would do.

For further thought, prayer and reflection

• Why is the wilderness a dangerous place as well as a great place?
• Have you developed a victim mentality in the wilderness? If so, what can you do to change this situation?
• Have you stopped praying due to being offended by the actions of someone else?
• Are you blaming other people for your situation, or will you take responsibility for it yourself?
• Have been relying too much on the prayers of others for breakthrough

in your own situation? Is it time for you to cry out to God in order to receive your own miracle?

Notes

1. clgillmore.com.
2. clgillmore.com.
3. Mosab Hassan Yousef, *Son of Hamas* (Milton Keynes: Authentic, 2011).
4. www.josephprince.org/daily-grace/

Twenty:
Loved by God

God loves each of us as if there were only one of us.
(St Augustine)[1]

Having little standing after being evicted from Pharaoh's palace and then thrown out of Abraham's home, Hagar had no influence, no power and no voice. For a period of time she was a forgotten woman; forgotten in Canaan and even in history. Centuries later, however, the voice of Hagar speaks more profoundly than ever to our own troubled generation.

So often we overlook great characters such as Hagar in the Bible and, instead, concentrate on other more prominent personalities. It's so easy to focus on Abraham and his extraordinary life of prayer or on Sarah the mother of Isaac, but what about Hagar and her son, Ishmael? What about these two unsung heroes whose lives continue to echo through the eras, causing us to examine our consciences and our motives? Who will relay their message and who will tell their story?

Perhaps there's no better generation to chronicle events in the life of Hagar than our own. After all, we are 'the social media kids' – a generation where prominence and platform is given to individual voices. Because the Bible contains so many heroic and fascinating stories, there are many voices in the Bible which have been relegated, causing these to be forgotten or ignored. I believe the story of Hagar is one such voice.

The voice of Hagar is still crying in the wilderness – but that voice is no longer a desperate one seeking food, shelter and survival; instead, her voice is a victorious one with a message of love and hope for the world. Her voice speaks of the true, unconditional and phenomenal love of God which can reach us in the most isolated of places. Her voice is saying:

God sees, God hears and God understands.

His is the voice of hope, the anchor of our souls. When there seems to be no way, He makes a way in any wilderness.

In this diverse world, where intolerance has led to much violence and despair, where mixed messages have caused extreme confusion and consternation, Hagar's story and voice proclaims hope for all peoples and nations, especially if they will turn to the true and living God who sees them in their sorrow.

Granted, Hagar may not have been particularly important in the grand scheme of things, but her life was important to God and her voice and message still resounds today.

Remember, Hagar was a slave, which means she wasn't free. Does this mean that Hagar, who is mostly forgotten, is actually more important than we would otherwise assume? In our eagerness to highlight the 'big players' in the Bible, have we missed the whole point of her life, which is to lead us to the unconditional love of God?

The story of Hagar has an important message to convey to us, especially in the way her life was divinely interrupted while she was in Egypt – and in the consequences which followed her years of subjection, Hagar's voice is telling us that God loves us no matter what circumstances we find ourselves in and, more than this, He wants to help deliver us from all of our troubles, just as He delivered both Hagar and Ishmael. Hagar represents many poor and abandoned souls in our world today. People who have been abused, rejected and even murdered by their fellow human beings. People who desperately require a voice of hope crying in their wilderness. Christians, Muslims, Mormons, Hindus and people of all cultures fall into this category. Slaves, foreign immigrants and refugees do also. A question we might ask today is: What is Hagar's voice saying to these groups and, more importantly, what does her voice have to say to our own generation?

Hagar was exceptionally loved by God. He proved this by responding to the voice of her young son while they were both at rock bottom in the wilderness. The Bible says: 'And God heard the voice of the lad; and the angel of God called to Hagar out of heaven, and said unto her, What aileth thee, Hagar? fear not; for God hath heard the voice of the lad where he is. Arise, lift up the lad, and hold him in thine hand; for I will make him a great nation' (Genesis 21:17,18).

This inheritance through Ishmael is evident today throughout the world and the Middle East. These are Muslims – the descendants of Ishmael. They are a seed of Abraham.

Significantly, God did not forget, nor neglect them. They are loved by God. Why? Because God cares for and blesses everyone unconditionally and equally. God hears the voice of those who cry out to Him. Whether they are Muslims or Christians, or any other religious grouping, God is interested in His creation. They are all loved by Him with an everlasting love. In the words of Augustine: *'God loves each of us as if there were only one of us.'*[2]

God promised not only to bless Isaac, but Ishmael, too and he kept his promise to both Hagar and Abraham regarding making nations out of the two boys.

Hagar's story has two momentous messages to relay. Firstly, following the mistakes made by Abraham and Sarah regarding the conception of Ishmael, God still blessed them all in their mess, and made something beautiful out of their mistakes.

In other words, God brought good out of a bad situation. He also proved how much He loved Hagar by coming to her aid when no one else cared. In His mercy and grace, not once did he ever abandon either her or Ishmael. On the contrary, we are informed that 'God was with the boy as he grew up' (Genesis 21:20, NIV 1984).

God may have appeared to have sided with Sarah, but the reality is, God gave the child of Sarah's handmaid a bright future, too, by first saving him from a certain death in the wilderness and then by allowing Ishmael to grow into a skilled hunter who eventually married 'one of his own' (an Egyptian) and became a father many times over.

This overwhelming evidence of God's unconditional love should bring hope to many of us. God is love. He didn't need Hagar. He wanted her. And that's what's so amazing!

It doesn't matter what you have done, where you have been, which religion you chose to believe in – or don't believe in – or even what people have told you about God. Hagar's voice is telling us all how God is a loving and compassionate God, and His love wants to draw you to Himself through the blood and sacrifice of Jesus Christ, God's Son.

Once we become a child of God we discover He's a loving and good Father to all. The Bible states: 'The eternal God is your refuge, and underneath are the everlasting arms' (Deuteronomy 33:27). Too often this scripture is read only at funerals, like Psalm 23, but God is not just our refuge in death, but also in life. He wants and is able to meet our needs now. Hagar's voice tells us that God can do the same for you and me as He did for Hagar and Ishmael. We are not perfect, of course, and many times we're even impetuous and downright impatient, just like Abraham and Sarah were, but God loves us and He understands and is willing to persevere with us. When we make mistakes, or find ourselves in trouble, God remains faithful in the same way He did for Hagar and her son.

Secondly, God's love was demonstrated for Hagar when He supernaturally provided for her in her own wilderness. Just when she assumed both she and Ishmael were going to die, bringing tears to her eyes and pain to her heart, God miraculously stepped in.

Wandering in a wilderness of grief and with no provision, she was stripped of everything – her safety, well-being, respect and standing. She was literally lying in the dust with no one to lean on except God Himself. Destitute and disillusioned beyond anything most people could ever imagine, suddenly, the Bible tells us, God provided a well of water for Hagar in her wilderness. 'Then God opened her eyes and she saw a well of water. So she went and filled the skin with water and gave the boy a drink' (Genesis 21:19, NIV 1984).

There are many examples in Scripture of how God came to people and opened their eyes to see, not just physically, but spiritually, one of the most notable spiritual occasions being the story of when Jesus met the woman at the well in John chapter

4. While we don't know her name or age, her conversation is one of the longest individual chats recorded in the Bible. She was a Samaritan woman and so her circumstances indicated she would be an unlikely convert. That's why I have used it as an illustration of God's love to the nations.

On a blistering hot day, Jesus stopped by a well for a rest and refreshment. It was Jacob's well outside the town of Sychar. A woman approached him holding a water jug and Jesus asked her, 'Will you give me a drink?' This question broke all the normal rules of custom. Firstly, the Jews would not readily have spoken to Samaritans due to bitter rivalry. Imagine the hatred between Israelis and Palestinians in Jerusalem and the Middle East, the enmity between Catholics and Protestants in Northern Ireland or the feuding between street gangs in Los Angeles or New York, and you have some idea of the feeling and its causes between Jews and Samaritans in the time of Jesus. Both politics and religion were involved. Secondly, men were not permitted to speak to woman without their husbands present, and thirdly rabbis were not expected to address women alone. But Christ was prepared to take risks in order to reach this woman's soul. She asked, 'You are a Jew and I am a Samaritan woman. How can you ask me for a drink?' (John 4:9, NIV 1984). Note how she focused on the law, while Jesus focused on grace. Jesus simply replied: 'If thou knewest the gift of God, and who it is that saith to thee, Give me to drink; thou wouldest have asked of him, and he would have given thee living water' (John 4:10).

In other words, Jesus offered her living water instead of her pouring Him a drink of earthly water. It's usually quite easy to find earthly water, but finding living water is something altogether different. Now Jesus had the lady's attention. But the woman was still inquisitive and continued the debate: 'Sir, thou hast nothing to draw with, and the well is deep: from whence then hast thou that living water?' (John 4:11).

Unlike many believers, who get upset and are uncomfortable when others ask questions about their faith, Jesus refused to panic. He had the answers. There was no need to be proud, arrogant or even nervous. Firstly He gave her an explanation about the fallibility of earthly water, stating: 'Whosoever drinketh of this water shall thirst again' (John 4:13). Then He added: 'But whosoever drinketh of the water that I shall give him shall never thirst; but the water that I shall give him shall be in him a well of water springing up into everlasting life' (John 4:14).

In this one sentence Christ moved from things temporal to things eternal. After exposing the fact that she previously had many husbands and was now living with someone else, Jesus showed Himself to be not only a prophet, but God's anointed One. He had come to a Samaritan woman who was viewed as being very much on the outside in order to reach her and bring her inside of His great covenant. No wonder she left that scene and is today recognised as one of the first evangelists, saying: 'Come, see a man who told me everything I ever did. Could this be the Christ?' (John 4:29, NIV 1984).

God cared about this woman's soul in the same way He cared for Hagar's soul. He was there for her when she was on the outside. He was – and still is – bigger than any nation, language, culture or creed.

Try to picture Hagar, someone who was born and raised in the land of Egypt, with its numerous false gods, who neither see nor hear, and now she is confronted by the living God, hearing His voice speaking to her in a remote wilderness, and supernaturally providing for all of her needs. She not only hears the voice of God, but the same God is concerned enough about her enough to send not one, but two angels her way.

God knows who she is – 'Hagar, Sarah's maid' (Genesis 16:8) – and now He has found her for the second time in her life in a barren desert. Just like He did when she fled from the mistreatment of her mistress, Sarah, and headed back towards the only other home she knew, the land of her birth, Egypt, so God has been following every one of Hagar's burning steps. God had made a way in the wilderness for a single woman without friends, family and resources to help her. He had seen, He had heard, He had provided and been faithful.

It seems doubtful that a young woman could have in fact survived the harsh and unforgiving wilderness, not once, but twice, through which she journeyed alone without supplies, but survive she most certainly did. Even as she lay fatigued and unaccompanied in the middle of a lonely oasis in a vast wasteland, she probably felt that no one in the entire world cared whether she lived or died, yet God cared and reached out to her in this desolate place.

There was a purpose in her pain – to reveal the immense love of the true and living God. Similarly, it was also during my own pain that I met with a loving God and visualised this book. In my times of distress I saw the story of Hagar afresh. When the cold winds of unemployment, rejection, homelessness, starvation and loss of status and power blow in like a hurricane, suddenly narratives like Hagar's take on a completely different meaning. We often find God more in the valley than on the mountaintops; we feel His presence and experience His helping hand more in our pain than in our gain.

God provided for Hagar a well of water. She was loved by God – a God who rescued her in her darkest hour. Perhaps more than anything, this is what makes Hagar a heroine for millions of people who are treading the same precarious path – a path I, too, have trodden. You see, what God did for Hagar gives all of us hope that He can do exactly the same for you and me!

For further thought, prayer and reflection

- What message is Hagar's story relaying to our generation?
- If Hagar, a rejected and spurned slave can survive, do you think it's possible that you, too, can make it, especially if you are a child of God?
- Do you view all Muslims as the enemies of God, or do you consider them to be people God loves and wants to save just as much agnostics, atheists and people of other religions?
- Can God bring good out of our bad situations? If so, how did this work in the life of Hagar and Ishmael? Has God ever provided a well of water for you in the wilderness – in other words, have you received your own special miracle? If so, have you gone out and told others about the goodness of God in your own life? Have you ever really considered how amazing it is that Hagar and Ishmael survived alone in the wilderness?

Notes

1. brainyquote.com.
2. brainyquote.com.

Twenty-one:
Forgiveness Helps Us Move Forward

In the shadow of my hurt, forgiveness feels like a decision to reward my enemy. But in the shadow of the cross, forgiveness is merely a gift from one undeserving soul to another.
(Andy Stanley)[1]

Of all the despicable deeds perpetrated by humankind, the Holocaust still ranks as arguably the most inconceivable. The Holocaust raises ethical questions that linger through history – one being, how do we forgive heinous crimes carried out against us by our fellow human beings? Is this even possible? And even if we can forgive, surely we cannot ever forget?

Just how did the survivors of the Holocaust react in the aftermath of that atrocity? Apparently they coped by carrying on as normal. Rabbi Jonathan Sacks states in *Not in God's Name*:

For decades they did not speak about the past, even to their spouses, even to their children. They focused single-mindedly on the future. They learned the language and culture of their new home. They worked and built careers. They married and had children. Only when they felt their future absolutely secure, forty or fifty years on, did many of them allow themselves to turn back and remember the past.[2]

Sacks added: 'The lesson they have taught society is: "First you have to build the future. Only then can you revisit the past without being held captive by the past".'[3]

Yet somewhere in between all of this must have been immense forgiveness, too, not to mention understanding. What event has visited your life that seems impossible to forgive? It may not seem like it, but it is possible to forgive even the worst offences. Corrie Ten Boom said: 'Forgiveness is an act of the will, and the will can function regardless of the temperature of the heart.'[4]

Ishmael's legacy is not solely that he survived a life of severe rejection and weariness in the wilderness of Beersheba; I believe his legacy is also found in his amazing ability to forgive his father and to find reconciliation with his brother, Isaac. Compassion was his greatest strength. His legacy exhorts us to forgive, forget and move forward with our lives, no matter what has befallen us.

In many ways, Ishmael's gesture of forgiveness and his attempts at reconciliation are what he should be most remembered for. He proved he was not a victim, but a victor. Why? Because forgiveness removes hate and frees the human spirit to build and love again, just like the survivors of the Holocaust managed to do.

To forgive is not easy, of course, especially when the crimes committed against us affect us personally, and our families. Some find the strength to forgive, while others do not. But if we cannot or do not willingly forgive, it hinders our progress and stops us from moving forward.

Zig Ziglar wrote: 'Look back in forgiveness, forward in hope, down in compassion and up with gratitude.'[5]

There is power in the act of forgiveness. Vincent Uzomah, a practising Christian and supply teacher at Dixons Kings Academy Bradford was stabbed in an unprovoked attack by a fourteen-year-old boy, but said later he totally forgave his assailant. That raises an interesting thought. Not being willing to forgive when something unspeakable happens to us is quite easy to understand, but people have trouble comprehending Vincent Uzomah's willingness to forgive. Earlier in this book I mentioned the story of assassin Dylann Roof who gunned down worshippers at the Charleston Emanuel African Methodist Episcopal Church. Yet this same congregation demonstrated extraordinary forgiveness towards their assailant following the shootings – an act of clemency which spoke to the entire world.

After his death, numerous tributes followed on behalf of the Reverend Clementa Pinckney, the senior pastor of the Charleston church, who was shot and killed by Roof, many recalling his non-confrontational style of ministry. Despite being offered numerous opportunities to engage in debate in relation to highly emotive issues during his life, the pastor mainly refused such invitations because he believed peace and love, not strife and hatred was the way to win people to God.

This approach is not only refreshing, it's also extremely biblical. The apostle Paul wrote in the first book of Corinthians, 'But earnestly desire the best gifts. And yet I show you a more excellent way' (1 Corinthians 12:31, NKJV), a reference to how love and forgiveness was the key to effective witnessing and to the winning of people's hearts. Paul was teaching that in order to make our position more successful, the more excellent way of love and forgiveness between all cultures would be required.

Genuine forgiveness is described as the final form of love. There is no love without forgiveness, and there is no forgiveness without love. Forgiveness doesn't excuse their behaviour; forgiveness prevents their behaviour from destroying your heart. Bearing no ill will is the starting point of true forgiveness because slowly, in time, God's grace can help all of us forgive; even the most atrocious of crimes.

Sometimes the word 'forgiveness' is used as though it's a natural thing, but many struggle to forgive. C.S. Lewis said, 'Forgiveness is a lovely idea until they have something to forgive.'[6] Nevertheless, forgiving one another is God's way, and if we remain unforgiving, the only person we end up hurting can be ourselves.

Forgiveness is one of the rudimentary principles of the Christian faith. Even when the Lord's Prayer is spoken we ask God to 'forgive those who have trespassed against us'.

What a challenge this presents to both believers and non-believers alike. Many religions, including Christianity, would do well to revisit again the subject of reconciliation and forgiveness, certainly if violence and strife throughout the world is to decrease at both individual and national levels.

There is hope for nations and for individuals who turn to God and His offer of reconciliation.

There is no hope without it.

When we seek for settlement and resolution, even when our cultures and religions vastly differ, I believe God smiles. And, yes, even when others do not respond to our overtures of love and attempts to reconcile things, either at a national or personal level, forgiveness in our hearts is still possible to attain, and God will bless our efforts. God sees the heart and He knows when we have done everything we can to maintain unity. Paul admonishes us:

'be ye kind one to another, tenderhearted, forgiving one another, even as God for Christ's sake hath forgiven you. (Ephesians 4:32). It is better to suffer failure after long perseverance, than never to have tried. No doubt people have messed up and hurt us! But how many times have we also fallen far short of the mark and hurt them? God wants to help us forgive and forget and enjoy communion and fellowship not only with Him, but also with one another. God sees the heart and He knows when we have done everything we can to maintain unity.

There is much in-fighting today, not just in secular life, but sadly within religious organisations. In my own country of Northern Ireland, a peace process is in place, following years of political and religious violence; nevertheless, peace is still not a reality in the province of Ulster. Far too much bigotry, hatred and unforgiveness remains buried under the surface between Catholics and Protestants throughout the entire island – hatred which is now being extended towards foreign nationals and other religious groups.

While many people are making efforts to 'forgive and forget' – indeed, when it comes to peace, there are some wonderful 'bridge builders' in the land of Ireland – the efforts of these brave optimists are being restricted by those unwilling to face the pain of the past and lance the boil of religious hatred once and for all. Many issues are blamed today for the lack of progress at political level, but the truth is, the absence of the word 'sorry' is the real problem. 'Sorry' is a Bible word. It speaks of remorse and repentance. Many people use the word 'regret' instead of the word 'sorry', but this is not true repentance. The Bible tells us in the first epistle of John, 'If we confess our sins, he is faithful and just to forgive us our sins, and to cleanse us from all unrighteousness' (1 John 1:9).

'Sorry' does seem to be the hardest word to say, yet the word 'sorry' leads to true repentance, and peace happens in the absence of hate.

James Arthur Baldwin said: 'I imagine one of the reasons people cling to their hates so stubbornly is because they sense, once hate has gone, they will be forced to deal with pain.'[7] And not only their pain, but their hatred also. Many religious groups today are filled with hatred. Their hate is so intense they even hate themselves. They are fighting for freedom, but hatred holds them in continual bondage. We cannot hope to experience a free society when hate is so visible. Bitterness, wrath, humiliation, a sense of loss and wrong all contribute to a distinct lack of freedom.

Albert Einstein wrote: 'Peace cannot be kept by force; it can only be achieved by understanding.'[8] True peace and reconciliation requires fortitude and forgiveness. Backing down, saying sorry, and recognising that one is wrong or has been wronged, takes courage and humility.

Ghandi said: 'The weak can never forgive. Forgiveness is the attribute of the strong.'[9] Nelson Mandela is quoted as saying: 'Forgiveness liberates the soul; it removes fear – that is why it is such a powerful weapon.'[10] Forgiveness produces a sense of release, and ultimately relief. It is not easy, but if we remain unforgiving we are the ones who suffer'. Alan Cohen wrote: 'You have the power to take away someone's happiness by refusing to forgive. That someone is you.'[11]

Real freedom for the human race comes when anger is replaced by both reconciliation and forgiveness. In order to be free, we have to forgive the past and embrace a new future and let go of the paralysis of hate. So vital is this principle of letting go and looking forward, Paul wrote in the book of Philippians: 'this one thing I do, forgetting those things which are behind, and reaching forth unto those things which are before, I press toward the mark for the prize of the high calling of God in Christ Jesus' (Philippians 3:13,14).

Sadly many people are not willing to 'turn the other cheek' as Jesus recommended; instead, they prefer the tactic of retaliation against those who have deeply hurt them. These hurts can last a lifetime and some people are even willing to go to their grave without being able to forgive.

The Sermon on the Mount is still the greatest sermon ever preached, and by the greatest preacher who ever lived – the Lord Jesus Christ. In it, Jesus constantly reminds us to love and forgive our enemies. While this is a noble goal, it is a most difficult one to accomplish. Yet Christ knew that without forgiveness no one can truly move on. Forgiveness is the way of God and the way of the cross. Even as Christ was being crucified by his own people He prayed: 'Father, forgive them; for they know not what they do' (Luke 23:34).

Forgiveness is always made easier for the Christian when we realise that God in Christ has also forgiven us. When we accept that we, too, didn't deserve mercy or forgiveness, yet have received it through Christ's blood at the cross, it is then by God's great grace we find it possible to forgive our perpetrators.

Andy Stanley wrote: 'In the shadow of my hurt, forgiveness feels like a decision to reward my enemy, but in the shadow of the cross, forgiveness is merely a gift from one undeserving soul to another.'[12]

Forgiveness is a huge subject, of course, and certainly one in which the Bible is not silent. In the Bible we read about a loving heavenly Father who forgives all of our trespasses. God calls sinners to seek Him and promises them forgiveness. Jesus extends a loving invitation for forgiveness of sins which is only possible through His shed blood at the cross of Calvary. Because Jesus was forsaken we can find forgiveness. Isn't this an awesome love?

The Bible says: 'In him we have redemption through his blood, the forgiveness of our trespasses, according to the riches of his grace, which he lavished upon us, in all wisdom and insight making known to us the mystery of his will, according to his purpose, which he set forth in Christ as a plan for the fullness of time, to unite all things in him, things in heaven and things on earth' (Ephesians 1:7–10, ESV).

Jesus taught that those who follow Him will love and forgive their enemies and reach out to other religions, as He also did. Nonetheless, in the face of excessive provocation by modern-day terrorists, I accept this is a difficult road for Christians to travel; nevertheless, God wants His children to show mercy, grace and love to their enemies in order to win them to God. Jesus is calling His children to forgive not only their friends, but also their enemies: 'Ye have heard that it hath been said, Thou shalt love thy neighbour, and hate thine enemy. But I say unto you, Love your enemies, bless them that curse you, do good to them that hate you, and pray for them which despitefully use you, and persecute you' (Matthew 5:43¬,44). Jesus also stated: 'For if you forgive men when they sin against you, your heavenly Father will also forgive you' (Matthew 6:14, NIV 1984).

One of the most powerful and moving acts of compassion the province of Ulster has possibly ever witnessed during the period known as the Troubles involved the late senator Gordon Wilson, whose daughter Marie was killed by a Provisional IRA bomb in the town of Enniskillen, Co. Fermanagh, Northern Ireland.

On 8 November 1987, the bomb exploded during Enniskillen's Remembrance Day parade, leaving Mr Wilson badly injured and fatally injuring his daughter Marie, who was a nurse. Mr Wilson recalled that the very last words he heard his daughter say were, 'Daddy, I love you very much.' Despite initially being unable to forgive the killers of his daughter on that never to be forgotten day in Northern Ireland's regrettable history, Gordon Wilson said: 'I have lost my daughter and we shall miss her, but I bear no ill will. I bear no grudge. Dirty sort of talk is not going to bring her back to life.'[13]

I vividly remember those words being spoken on television by Gordon Wilson. I wasn't a Christian at the time and I was full of anger and rage, having witnessed many of my fellow countrymen blown to pieces by terrorists. In my unforgiving state, I even recollect screaming out my total disapproval at how Gordon Wilson had found the strength to forgive, not hate, in the face of such dreadful grief and provocation. Only later when I gave my own heart to Jesus Christ did I fully understand why he was able to pardon the killers of his daughter – it was because of the grace of Almighty God working in him.

Today many believe the violence being carried out by Islamic extremists should be countered by further violence through military action, but there is a better option available to evangelicals in their response to this recognisable modern-day challenge.

The first thing Jesus did when conflict arose in His own generation was to try to establish some form of peace, not war. Jesus not only taught His disciples to be peacemakers, He told them that if they embraced peace they could claim to be genuine followers of God, saying: 'Blessed are the peacemakers: for they shall be called the children of God' (Matthew 5:9). Jesus was simply saying if we claim to be the children of God, genuine lovers of peace and not war, we would become exactly like God. We can never earn the right to be called the children of God; it is a gift, grace we don't deserve, but as we surrender to God we inevitably become more like Him, even in relation to peace.

But what about people who have been inhumanly attacked and suffered enormous loss at the hands of terrorists? How, for example, do Israeli, Christian, Palestinian, Arab and Muslim families come to terms with the brutal slaying of their loved ones across the Middle East and elsewhere? How is it possible to forgive then? Of ourselves, it is not possible; only God's grace can truly enable this transformation of heart, but the challenge for all of us is still to respond in peace, love and forgiveness. Alexander Pope said: 'To err is human; to forgive, divine.'[14]

The Holocaust survivors are inspirational examples that it is possible to at least move forward and build a new life. Gordon Wilson proved that forgiveness is possible in the face of immense personal grief. Vincent Uzomah chose the way of forgiveness in order to help him move on and liberate his thoughtless persecutor.

Ishmael, however, did exactly the same thing. He became an expert with the bow and Hagar managed to secure a wife for him; and, of course, God had promised Hagar during her first spell in the wilderness that He would make a great nation out of Ishmael.

While we don't know whether Hagar ever saw Abraham and Sarah again after their infamous separation, we are enlightened as to possible reconciliation between Ishmael and Isaac following Abraham's death. As unlikely as it seemed, Ishmael and Isaac would stand shoulder to shoulder together again and, as is so often the case, they were reunited in the midst of death, sorrow and even remorse. What had made this unlikely reunion possible? Forgiveness! Forgiveness doesn't change the past, but it helps broaden the future. It makes it possible for us to move on.

For further thought, prayer and reflection

- Can we choose to forgive or not?
- Are you carrying some form of unforgiveness against your brother or sister or someone who has brought harm to you?
- What is the root cause of unforgiveness?
- Can forgiving people enhance individual relationships and increase the prosperity of a nation?
- Why does God want us to forgive one another?

Notes

1. goodreads.com.
2. Rabbi Jonathan Sacks, *Not in God's Name* (London: Hodder & Stoughton, 2015), p. 243.
3. Sacks, *Not in God's Name*.
4. Goodreads.com.
5. ziglar.com.
6. sermonquotes.com.
7. brainyquote.com.
8. brainyquote.com.
9. goodreads.com.
10. *Invictus*, 2009, indb.com
11. goodreads.com.
12. goodreads.com.
13. consolations.com.
14. brainyquote.com.

Twenty-two:
We'll Be Together Again

*Reconciliation means working together to correct the legacy of
past injustice. (Nelson Mandela)*[1]

Not many relationships survive major fallout. No matter how
hard we try to resurrect what we once enjoyed with a loved
one, friend or colleague, the fact is, deep wounds destroy
relationships. Trust dies. So does love. That doesn't mean some
form of reconciliation isn't possible, however.

One of the Bible's most infamous fallouts which still managed
to end in some form of settlement happened between the mighty
apostle Paul and the gentle encourager, Barnabas. Their separation
was extremely sad because both were ministers of the gospel, and
it is never appropriate for two such men to be divided.

Paul, who had previously been called Saul of Tarsus had,
prior to his conversion, been a persecutor of Christians
and wasn't trusted by believers, even following his notable
transformation. Despite Paul's miraculous change on the

Damascus Road, Barnabas had to persuade the disciples to let the apostle fellowship with them. As a result of this intervention, a wonderful friendship between Paul and Barnabas was then formed. However, during their first missionary journey together, John Mark, the cousin of Barnabas, who had accompanied them, chose to return to Jerusalem for reasons we do not know. Later when Barnabas suggested bringing John Mark on another planned journey, Paul strongly opposed the idea.

The Bible records in Acts chapter 15 that a 'sharp contention' developed between the two, and eventually they went their separate ways. Barnabas took Mark and sailed for Cyprus, while Paul chose Silas and left, commended by believers to the grace of the Lord.

The question since has frequently been, who was right and who was wrong?

Some lean towards Paul on the issue because afterwards he appeared to be the more prominent one, but Barnabas continued to work quietly for God in the background and his spirit of love and compassion towards John Mark only contributed to his reputation as a great encourager and evangelist. The fact is, God loved both of these dedicated evangelists. This wasn't a doctrinal, but a personal dispute.

Certainly, it does seem harsh that Paul couldn't overlook what he evidently saw as a failing by John Mark earlier and allow him another chance. After all, who among us would not welcome another opportunity to prove ourselves to God? That's assuming, of course, John Mark needed another chance at all because there is no record of him doing anything wrong – only in Paul's opinion. Drumbeat of Love by Lloyd Ogilvie stated: 'Paul had fought and won one of history's most crucial battles over the Gentile converts. He was not able, however, to apply the same truth to his relationship with John Mark'[2] at least, not until much later, when we glimpse more than a hint of reconciliation between the pair.

Something must have transpired in the intervening years to bring these men together again, because Paul had a distinct change of heart about John Mark. Time has a way of mellowing us all. In the second book of Timothy, Paul wrote: 'Only Luke is with me. Get Mark and bring him with you, because he is helpful to me in the ministry' (2 Timothy 4:11, NIV 1984). When did this softening by the apostle Paul take place? What changed his mind about Mark? There is no record that Paul or Barnabas ever saw one another again after their infamous parting, but forgiveness and reconciliation is still apparent in this narrative, especially when we examine in more detail the words of Paul in the book of Timothy.

Further evidence of their reconciliation comes in Colossians chapter 4, a long time after the events which took place in Acts chapter 15, when the Colossian church is encouraged to give Mark a hearty welcome. The verse records: 'Aristarchus my fellow prisoner wishes to be remembered to you, as does Mark the relative of Barnabas. You received instructions concerning him; if he comes to you give him a [hearty] welcome' (Colossians 4:10, Amplified Version).

Initially Paul hadn't seen eye to eye with Barnabas regarding John Mark, but he was not only eventually reconciled, he then recommends Mark to the churches, which is evidence of a truly forgiving Christian spirit.

Matthew Henry's commentary states: 'If men have been guilty of a fault it must not always be remembered against them. We must forgive and forget.'[3]

I mention the above illustration in relation to reconciliation because I believe the same spirit of settlement which was apparent in Paul is equally manifest in Abraham's first son, Ishmael. From all that I've read about the story of Hagar and Ishmael, nothing has challenged me more than Ishmael's own gesture of reconciliation found in the words in Genesis chapter 25. Describing events at the burial of Abraham, the Bible records: 'And his sons Isaac and Ishmael buried him in the cave of Machpelah, in the field of Ephron the son of Zohar the Hittite, which is before Mamre' (Genesis 25:9).

Think about it!

Ishmael, the once young teenager abandoned by his father Abraham and left to die in the wilderness of Beersheba with his mother, Hagar, still turns up at his father's funeral many years later. If what happened to Ishmael had happened to you or me, would we have been in attendance at our father's burial site? It is a challenging question.

Ishmael and Isaac, who quite possibly hadn't spoken two words together from the time both Hagar and Ishmael were separated from the family home, are somehow reunited at the funeral of their father, Abraham. This reunion would surely have been harder for Ishmael than Isaac, of course.

After all, throughout his life Isaac was lavished with love and constant care in the family home by his father, Abraham; he never knew what it was like to endure the wilds of the wilderness or fear for the future in the same way his brother, Ishmael, had experienced. So, attendance at his father's burial would have been completely natural for Isaac. Ishmael, on the other hand, along with his mother, had been cast out of his father's house as a young boy, given nothing more than a bottle of water and a loaf of bread – and may never have been seen or heard from again. Had God not rescued him and Hagar by that well in the wilderness, both of them would surely have died.

As mentioned earlier, the Bible doesn't tell us whether Hagar ever saw Abraham and Sarah after she and Ishmael were exiled from the family all those years beforehand. The last we see of Hagar, in fact, is when she's living in the Desert of Paran, in the Sinai Peninsula, busy securing a wife and therefore a future for Ishmael.

Yet the mere fact that Ishmael attended his father's funeral suggests that, just like Paul, Mark and Barnabas, reconciliation of some sort may have taken place within the family in the intervening years, even if only in the heart of Ishmael.

Imagine the random comments and nudging of one another as Ishmael arrives at the burial site.

'Apparently that's Ishmael, the brother of Isaac.'

'He's got so old, I wouldn't have known him.'

'After what Abraham did to him, I wouldn't be within a million miles of here.'

'He's a braver man than me.'

'I know, but I admire him; it must be hard to forgive and forget all that stuff.'

Visualise, too, the stares, the looks Ishmael might have received from people still not able to forgive him for the mocking of his brother, Isaac. He'd gone out in in disgrace, remember, accompanied by his mother, Hagar, and people have long memories, don't they?

I wonder what went through the mind of Ishmael as he stood side by side with his brother at the burial of Abraham. Did the painful memories of all those years before suddenly spring to mind? Did he feel hurt and disappointment at how his father had treated him? Did he wish he was somewhere else? Or did he stand there in total forgiveness, regardless of what had taken place? Surely he had regrets, yet the fact that he was there at all suggests Ishmael had dealt with them. It reveals him as a man of character and of forgiveness. It indicates that reconciliation and clemency was more important to him than recrimination.

This provokes an important question. Are we like Ishmael? When things don't go as planned with our own loved ones and brethren, when separation occurs, are we able to forgive and forget – or do we remain bitter, angry, unforgiving and separated for the rest of our lives?

Some relationships are not repairable, of course, but reconciliation is still possible if we are willing to forgive. No matter what has taken place, God's way is the way of peace, restoration and reconciliation. The truth is, genuine reconciliation only comes through the atoning blood of Jesus Christ. Paul declared in the second book of Corinthians: 'And all things are of God, who hath reconciled us to himself by Jesus Christ, and hath given to us the ministry of reconciliation' (2 Corinthians 5:18).

It would be over seventy years from the time Ishmael found himself exiled in the wilderness to his return to his father's funeral in the field of Ephron. Interestingly, Ishmael didn't appear to revisit his own painful past until many years later when he turned up at Abraham's funeral, by which time he had, of course, already built a new life, got married and was viewed as a skilled archer. We often require time to heal from great hurts and when this happens reconciliation can become a reality. Some reunions have broken down because the wounds were still too raw and the pain too deep for genuine unity to take place, but the time was now right for Ishmael and Isaac.

Imagine Isaac and Ishmael's reaction to one another, assuming they hadn't spoken since that notorious day when Ishmael was exiled from the home. What an awkward setting it must have been. Did they embrace each other, or stand at a distance? Did they apologise to one another? Or did they acknowledge one another in a civil and even loving manner?

The fact that Ishmael was present is what really gave reconciliation a chance. Sometimes just the smallest gesture is all that is required to start the process of reconciliation. A phone call, a card, a visit, a text message, a kind word to someone about the person who hurt you or whom you hurt is all it may take to begin the relationship again.

We will never know if saving a relationship is possible unless we try, and have the courage to make the first move. The way of peace and reconciliation is one of the most critical and creative of human actions.

Notably Ishmael not only went and helped bury his father, he buried the past with him. I'm not suggesting it was easy for Ishmael to either forget or forgive what had taken place in his life, but the gesture in attending his father's funeral makes him a truly great human being.

He probably wasn't expected to be present by many. Indeed, people would have understood if he hadn't shown up that day. But he did. He forgave his father and his brother and what's more, it's quite possible Isaac may well have also forgiven him.

One myth within Judaism enchantingly suggests that, after Sarah died, it was no coincidence that Isaac was living near Beer Lahai Roi, which, is, of course, the place where Hagar saw the 'well of the living One who sees me'. Some ancient scholars believe Isaac deliberately moved here with the sole intention of initiating reconciliation between his father, Abraham, with Hagar. Isaac might possibly have not only greatly desired to see reconciliation between Abraham and Hagar, but also between him and Ishmael. What had stopped this reunification previously? Could it be that while Sarah was alive this was not likely, but once she had passed away, things changed? The legend even implies that Abraham's new wife, Keturah, with whom he had six more sons, was actually Hagar.

Sadly, it is a fact that not until certain individuals pass away is true reconciliation often possible between broken people, and nations. Sometimes generations must pass in order for the liberty of God's Spirit to return.

Many rulers or leaders have exercised so much dominance and control they have ended up becoming a curse to their nation, organisation or even place of worship. By refusing to allow change to emerge it is not until they have passed away or been extricated from their positions that new horizons and fresh relationships prove possible.

It wasn't, for example, until the year King Uzziah died that Isaiah saw the Lord 'high and exalted' (Isaiah 6:1, NIV 1984). Not until the spirit of control is broken can true freedom, love and reconciliation emerge. There was peace and reconciliation between the brothers Isaac and Ishmael, because the stumbling block (Sarah) was now out of the picture and both boys were willing to reach out in their separate ways and both were prepared to work through issues from their past in order to be reconciled. The late Nelson Mandela once said: 'Reconciliation means working together to correct the legacy of past injustice.'[4]

Reconciliation still requires much effort, however, but the results make it worthwhile. Following our fallouts, forgiveness and reconciliation is the place where God wants us to travel. In the words of Edwin Louis Cole: 'The pattern of the prodigal is: rebellion, ruin, repentance, reconciliation and finally restoration.'[5]

As I conclude the remarkable story of Hagar and Ishmael, I wish to end on an exceptionally exciting and optimistic and perhaps prophetic note. If the once-squabbling Ishmael and Isaac are representative of the quarrelling religions of Islam and Christianity and Judaism today – and all the evidence seems to suggest that this is so; if the choice of Isaac over Ishmael is a picture of the contentions today relating to the promise of God between Judaism, Christianity and Islam – then wouldn't it follow that the sight of the two brothers standing side by side at their father's burial is something God allowed to happen in order to give us hope for the future?

Why can't we experience peace between opposing religions in this generation also, providing individuals look to the Prince of Peace, Jesus Christ – the only way of true peace and unity? It is not good enough to say there will be no peace until Jesus comes, which many people have done in order to justify a lack of effort or even willingness on their own part to make peace. Many hide behind this statement in an attempt to prevent them having to face the difficult issue of unity and reconciliation. Yet God wants us to become peacemakers now! And the spirit of peace is surely the evidence of a life lived for God. Psalm 34 exhorts the people of God to 'Turn from evil and do good; seek peace and pursue it' (Psalm 34:18, NIV 2011). Making peace with another religion is not being disloyal to Jesus. It is a starting point to discuss the differences between people of different backgrounds and then hopefully point them to the true and living God.

I believe the image of both Ishmael and Isaac standing side by side at their father's funeral serves as a thrilling prospect of possible peace and reconciliation to come between Abraham's children who, let's be honest, have been separated for far too long – a coming together, of course, of the three Abrahamic faiths *through the blood and sacrifice of the Lord Jesus Christ.*

This is more than wishful thinking, but entirely possible to experience. This is God's intention. Remember what Paul said: 'And all things are of God, who hath reconciled us to himself by Jesus Christ, and hath given to us the ministry of reconciliation' (2 Corinthians 5:18).

When peace is found in Christ, reconciliation is possible, and several other things can legitimately take place. For example, individuals who follow the three Abrahamic faiths – Islam, Christianity and Judaism – can finally be unified and become brothers again, but only if those same individuals are converted through the sacrifice, death and resurrection of Jesus Christ. God's Word clearly states that this is the only way of salvation. Jesus said so Himself in the book of John, declaring: 'I am the way and the truth and the life. No one comes to the Father except through me' (John 14:6). The book of Acts reiterates this, stating, 'Salvation is found in no one else, for there is no other name under heaven given to mankind by which we must be saved' (Acts 4:12, NIV 2011). When Jesus is received as Lord and Saviour by individuals, then the labels of Islam, Christianity and Judaism will finally drop off and all will be part of the family of God and known simply as the children of God.

When the children of Abraham and other religions of the world understand that God loves them unconditionally and desires to see them reconciled through the One Peter described as 'the Son of the living God' (John 6:69), the Lord Jesus Christ, then peace and blessing will surely follow in many homes, communities and nations around the world. Jesus and the message of Christianity is the answer to the conflict in the world today. Money is not the answer; neither is the wisdom of man. Only Christ can make the difference. Philip Yancey wrote:

'The Christian faith is ... basically about love and being loved and reconciliation. These things are so important, they're foundational and can transform individuals, and families.[6]

Ishmael and Isaac are an example of how forgiveness, reconciliation and peace are possible when people choose the way of God. Loving God does not mean hating the enemies of God; neither does loving the enemies of God mean we hate or are disloyal to our faith or God. This notion has already led to all kinds of chaos, violence and destruction.

Remember when the Israelites entered the Promised Land, Moses taught them not to hate. Instead he taught them to love those who had persecuted them. Why? He was advocating a better way because forgiveness, peace and reconciliation is God's ideal and has always been God's purpose for his creation.

Jesus is referred to in the Scriptures as the 'Prince of Peace' (Isaiah 9:6), and when the angel and heavenly host announced His birth it was with the words 'peace' and 'good will toward men' (Luke 2:14). The gospel is described as 'the gospel of peace' (Romans 10:15; Ephesians 6:15). Peace and reconciliation therefore is the fruit of love, not hate; it is the evidence of forgiveness, not unforgiveness. Reconciliation destroys hate and it helps wipe out unforgiveness. True reconciliation says, 'I'm sorry!', 'We're sorry!', 'Let's try again.'

One of the lessons from the book of Genesis is that: *not until people live in peace can any nation truly flourish. The message of this book is: loving our own is never enough; we must learn to love the Hagars of this world – those who feel unloved and rejected in society.*

Hagar's suffering and Ishmael's forgiveness is calling us to bury the past and live at peace with one another, regardless of what religion we belong to. Many apologies may be necessary by all sides, as the world attempts to put away its differences, but if this is the price of peace then the opportunity must be seized. After all, every one of us is made in the image of God, human beings created for His glory and for His great honour. If you have been left to die, remember, you are loved by a most loving and wonderful God – One who can find you and restore you, no matter what has taken place in your life.

For further thought, prayer and reflection

- What do you think happened to make the apostle Paul to change his mind about John Mark?
- Have you ever considered how amazing it is that Ishmael was able to stand at his father's graveside beside his brother, Isaac, despite what had taken place earlier in his life?
- Have you experienced a dreadful incident which has caused you much pain and stopped reconciliation between you and the other person? Are you willing to humble yourself in order to gain reconciliation with someone you have been separated from? What can you do to make the first move to establish contact again?
- Have you forgiven someone for hurting you, in an effort to experience true reconciliation?
- What is reconciliation the fruit of?
- What is the foundation of the Christian faith?

Notes

1. facebook.com.
2. christiancurrier.com.
3. Matthew Henry's Concise Commentary, biblehub.com.
4. thedailybeast.com.
5. brainyquote.com.
6. brainyquote.com.

Epilogue: An Amazing Encounter

There are some incidents with God which are simply unforgettable. These encounters often grab one by surprise. I refer to these supernatural events as 'God moments' or 'God set-ups'.

I have enjoyed many such encounters, especially prior to the publication of *Left to Die but Loved by God*.

My manuscript finally put to bed and, having agreed a late October release date with my London publisher, it was time to celebrate with a three-course meal. I didn't have far to travel. The well-known and highly popular Asian restaurant I'd chosen was located inside the hotel where I was staying in central London. But not so fast! It was fully booked and things didn't look good for a man seeking a single table on a frantic Friday night.

Never one to give up when it comes to Asian food, I waited them out and managed to secure a corner spot in the fashionable London eatery. I wasn't left disappointed, either. The chicken curry and fried rice was scrumptious, and hot, just the way I like it. It even included potatoes!

As I paid the bill, my intention was to retire to my room early. It had been a long day; yet something drove me outside for some fresh air and, lo and behold, there she was… a modern-day Hagar!

In fact, even before I had stepped out of the revolving doors of the hotel entrance, a striking but extremely tired-looking lady had somehow collapsed at my feet.

'Please, sir, may I have some change?' she pleaded.

'Of course you can, but what's going on with you?' I replied.

Angelica (not her real name) added, 'I'm homeless and have been for years now. I'm fifty and I'm just so tired, sir.'

'I'd prefer if you call me John. Have you eaten today?' I responded.

I knew she hadn't, so I invited her into the hotel for some food.

'What, in there, sir? Oh my goodness, no, I couldn't go in there.'

I saw the panic in her eyes. Her next comment not only challenged me; it made me quite angry. 'You will only get thrown out, sir, it's not worth it.'

My eyes filled to the brim. She didn't feel worthy to even step inside. I took her by the arm and brought her inside anyway. We walked to the hotel lounge which usually requires a reservation, but thankfully it had quietened down after a busy day of afternoon tea.

'Are you sure this is OK?' she insisted nervously.

'Trust me, it is more than OK, Angelica, you are my guest, and if they don't let us in I will simply check out and go somewhere else.'

The manager of the lounge was waiting at the door and proved accommodating, pointing to a window seat.

It transpired Angelica begged by day and slept at Heathrow Airport by night. 'I get the bus at the West End and it takes me to the airport. It's safe there and warm and there are other homeless people; you wouldn't believe how many,' she said.

We ordered tea, but with her hands trembling, she dripped most of it on the table and over her saucer. Life hadn't been kind to Angelica. Of course, she didn't realise I'd just spent the best part of a year churning out a book about social issues affecting our world today, including a spotlight on homeless people like her.

'It's a system, sir,' Angelica told me. 'I'm a single homeless person with no children, so I don't qualify for any benefits. Once you have no address and no real identity, no one wants to know you and you just get sucked into this way of life.'

During her youth, Angelica was a 100 and 200 metre champion sprinter, but after her alcoholic mother threw her out, she became desperate and couldn't cope. She once had several jobs as a secretary, but even these were taken from her.

I mentioned this book to her and what it was all about – namely, that God cares for the refugee, for the homeless, and that there is hope in Jesus, no matter what a person's situation. To my delight she then confessed that she, too, was a strong Christian and that she had previously been baptised. I was intrigued as she spoke knowledgably about the Scriptures and about her desire for a home in eternity one day with God.

The reality is, she had more faith than me. As I watched her face light up at the prospect of eternity with God, I knew she was a saved person and I also felt incredibly challenged by her extraordinary faith.

'Unless Jesus fixes it right for me, no one really cares. He is my only hope now,' she maintained.

At that moment I realised I was experiencing a 'God moment' – a 'God set-up' – and a truly amazing confirmation in relation to my book. Angelica reminded me of the lady I'd been writing about for months – the Egyptian woman called Hagar. Like Hagar,

Angelica had endured horrific hardship, yet still possessed a strong and determined spirit. She's a modern-day Hagar in every sense – a survivor and a truly inspirational person. Angelica, however, represents millions of other Hagars today who just need a chance and who are waiting on a miracle of their own.

'I'm fifty and I'm still here, that has to be God, sir… that has to be God!' Angelica insisted as we parted that evening.

I invited her for breakfast the following morning and, she turned up just as I was on my way to the restaurant. We shared scrambled eggs and toast and enjoyed interesting conversation, but our time was too short. We were both going to the airport that day for different reasons; yet what an amazing encounter!

Today I'm still in touch with Angelica. It's my prayer that she will be present for the launch of this book where she will receive a free copy and, who knows, find a well of water of her own, just when she thought it might never happen. Remember what God did for Hagar, and for Angelica – He can do for you.